The Room to Be Brave

Sometimes the way forward begins with going back.

April Day Garcia

First edition

ISBN: 979-8-9941343-1-3

Author's Note

Author's Note

Some names, identifying details, and circumstances have been changed to protect the privacy of individuals and to honor the boundaries of this story. The emotional truth of the experiences described remains unchanged.

The Room to Be Brave

Sometimes the way forward begins with going back.

April Day Garcia

Contents

For Rick and Bella

Rick, you showed me what it means to be chosen. Bella, you showed me what I was fighting for. This book is for you both—my home, my heart, my reason to be brave.

Prologue

I have written this book a thousand times: while blow-drying my hair, sitting in traffic, or lying awake at night, narrating it to myself like a confession I never quite finish.

I love to tell stories. But this story, my story? It's harder to tell. Sometimes I think if I tell it perfectly enough, it'll finally make sense.

It is impossible to tell my story without brushing against other people's wounds. And let me be clear: my intention is not to hurt anyone. That's one of the reasons it took me so long to put these words on paper. But knowing that people are flawed, especially me—*God, especially me*—I have come to a place where I can allow for imperfection. I can hold space for forgiveness and grace. I can see how people did what they did in a moment in time: that doing bad things and being a bad person are not necessarily the same.

I do not write from a high horse or moral high ground. I tell this story from the middle of the mess: the mess of recovery, of broken family patterns, of learning to choose differently. I write with full awareness that plenty of stories could be written where I am the villain.

As I walk you through the experiences that have shaped me, we will inevitably uncover traces of other people and their mistakes. Because we don't heal in isolation. We heal in context; in connection with the people who hurt us, loved us, or simply stood by while we figured ourselves out.

But this isn't their story. It's mine. I'm telling it the way I lived it, the way I remember it, the way I have learned to carry it.

If you happen to find pieces of your own story woven through mine, I hope you can offer me the same grace I'm still learning to give myself. Because that's all this really is: an act of grace, room by room.

Part One

The Castle I Carry

Every day I wake up tired.

Not the kind of tired that a good night's sleep can fix, but the kind that lives in your bones. The kind of tired that comes from carrying too much for too long.

I have spent my life carrying the weight of every room I have ever stood in. The room I was in when my first husband handed me a letter asking for a divorce. The room where the surgeon pulled the bandages off my hand, and I saw that three of my fingers were gone. The room where I found out I was pregnant with my daughter, sitting on the edge of my bed, staring at the two pink lines that would change everything.

Whether they are filled with joy, grief, laughter, or pain, each memory lives in the room where it all happened, in this castle I carry in my heart.

As I open one door I see the apartment I lived in with my mother and brother, when I was in the third grade. There was marbled carpet and a gas fireplace. That was the room where Child Protective Services interviewed my mother after I told the school she had slapped me across the face when I had the nerve to ask about dinner. I remember the weight of their questions; how official they were. How small I felt. I still, to this day, wonder how my mother carries that room.

The next door opens to a room with an old, worn leather couch. A couch that smelled faintly of smoke and someone else's life. It belonged to a man whose face I can't remember. I woke up on that couch with my shorts wet, disoriented after a long night of drinking. The morning light was too bright and my mouth tasted like shame. I had peed on a stranger's couch. I slipped out of that room and drove myself home in soiled shorts, never knowing whose living room I had just been in.

The next room opens into a tan-carpeted living room with a checkered brown couch and the dusty smell of unopened mail and old magazines. It was one of the few rooms in all of California where I felt safe. It's the room I was sitting in when I made the decision to leave the West Coast for good. Safety didn't sit right with me back then. I didn't know how to stay in it, so I ran.

Some rooms are inviting and soft to revisit and I love the memories I keep there; the laughter, the warmth, the comfort. I have even borrowed design elements from those rooms and brought them into my current home. Other rooms hold elements like fluted molding and southwestern décor that will never make it through my front door. They will remain in my memory, safely tucked away where they can't make me relive how I felt in their company.

We all carry these invisible rooms behind our smiles and beneath our to-do lists. Some people bolt the doors shut and never look in. They hide their rooms and what happened in them from the world, and even from themselves. Others leave them wide open, performing their pain like a sad show and tell.

Neither makes the house any lighter.

So, if closing the doors doesn't help lift the weight, nor does leaving them wide open, what the hell are we supposed to do?

Honestly? I don't know.

But maybe we start by walking through the rooms together... slowly, and honestly. Let's open a few windows and let in a little light. Maybe, somewhere in each room, we'll find the key that helps us release what has been weighing us down.

That's how I will tell my story.

Room by room, memory by memory. Not with perfection, but with grace. Not with a strength that never bends, but with the courage to walk back into every room that shaped me and see what I left behind—and what I'm ready to carry forward.

The Room That
Was Almost Mine

I sat on an old sofa with a crocheted throw across my lap. Across from me sat a woman with long brown hair and piercing brown eyes. She was in a faded orange chair; a yellow legal pad balanced on her knee.

This was my first psychic reading.

I didn't go because I believed in magic. I went because I needed to believe in something. At thirty-five, I was still trying to make sense of the drama of my life.

Why did all of these things happen to me, and what was I supposed to do with all of it?

The woman told me so many things in the hour we were together: that my daughter was an old soul (*true*), that I needed to work through my feelings about my mother (*also true*), and that I carried a lot of something she referred to as "karmic debt." She said I had spent my entire childhood and early twenties paying down a generational burden that wasn't mine. She told me that much of the work was already done and that it took a lot of strength for me to survive what I had and to still have the ability to shine.

Then the woman asked why I don't look at pictures from my childhood.

How the hell did she even know that? *Oh, right. Psychic.*

She told me to look at those pictures. To really see that little girl. That the little girl in those pictures was raised in a world that told her she was unlovable, and she refused to believe it. That the little girl not only endured but endured with joy in her heart. That I should be proud of her, and I should see her as the brave little girl she was.

The brave little girl she still is.

She gave me hope when she told me that the first and second halves of my life would look completely different.

She was so fucking right.

The first half began in June 1978, when my mother was just twenty years old. By then, she was already raising my brother, Brian, who was born the previous June. I arrived the day before his first birthday. My mother and father were not together very long. In fact, he was out of town and onto his next adventure before I even took my first breath.

I have six photographs of my father, maybe, if I'm being generous—more pictures than facts about him. He looks young, maybe twenty-six. He usually wears a t-shirt and jeans and has long brown curls flowing into a matching beard. He's tall, broad-shouldered, and in some photos, he's grinning ear to ear as he holds a baby. For years, I wanted to believe that the baby was me, that I was the one who made him smile so proudly. But the dates on the back of the photos tell the truth: the baby in his arms is Brian. There isn't a single picture of him smiling down at me.

My mother and I spent three days in the hospital while she recovered from her second c-section in under a year. For those three days she struggled to give her new baby girl a name, while the nurses tending to us would tell her that I couldn't be "Baby Girl" forever. She had to pick a name. So, in the middle of the night, in June, she did:

April Day.

Within days of giving me a name, my mother made the heartbreaking decision to give me up for adoption. She chose to raise my brother and sent me to live with strangers. I understand why, he was already a year old, already hers. But it still hurts.

I was adopted by a couple from Lake Tahoe, California, a firefighter and his wife. That's all I know for certain about the people who took me in, but in my imagination, I built them the most beautiful, cozy home, a place where I could feel safe and content.

My new parents were kind and supportive. We had an oak kitchen table where we ate dinner together every night. There was a brick fireplace with family photos on the mantel and an old dog that slept at the foot of my bed.

My mom listened to every story I told. She ran the PTA and was the leader of my Girl Scout troop. My father made pancakes on Sunday mornings. He got teary when I dressed up for the father-daughter dance and told me that if I worked hard enough, I could change the world.

I can still hear his slippers on the kitchen tile and feel the dog's weight against my legs. I can hear her humming while she irons a patch onto a sash that was never mine. It's a whole life I walk through sometimes, even though none of it ever happened.

None of it was real.

The reality was that just before the State of California finalized my adoption, my biological mother returned. She had a change of heart and refused to sign the papers. She showed up at the door and took me from the only home I had ever known. From the family who loved me for a year. All because she knew better.

She always did.

At a year old, I couldn't have understood what was happening. One day, I was with my parents; the next, I was living with a stranger. A one-year-old knows her mother's smell, her parents' routine, the rhythm of her home. Then, suddenly, without warning, all of that was taken away.

How long did I cry for them?

How long did they cry for me?

As I was growing up, I often wondered why I felt so disconnected from my biological mother. Seeing mothers and daughters on television, or spending time with my friends with their mothers, I never understood that easy bond, that warmth.

Was it me? Was I broken?

Why wasn't I connected to my mother the way other daughters seemed to be?

There must be a bond that forms in the very first year of life. One that I completely missed.

Or maybe I didn't miss it at all. Maybe I had it with someone else, and she's just... gone. I don't know her name. I don't know his name. I don't know where that connection went.

It's strange, carrying that knowledge. That there once was a bond, and now it's gone forever. I can't help but wonder, where does that part of me live now?

It must be tucked away in a room, hidden behind all the others. A room that's just out of reach, that my heart can't quite touch, but I know it's there.

What happened to the couple who thought their dreams had come true? They finally had their baby girl, only to lose her a year later. How the hell do you recover from that? Did they adopt again?

Who grew up in the room that used to be mine?

That room carries a missing link that can never be reconnected.

That should have been the last time my mother left and came back. It should have ended there: the leaving, the breaking, the rebuilding. But it didn't. There were so many times where I watched her walk away from me and eventually return. As the years went on, though, it got harder and harder to see her standing at the door.

But she kept coming back. And I kept letting her in.

The Room with
the Big Stick

My brother Brian was my best friend. He had blonde hair and blue eyes like our mother, with the cutest freckles scattered across the bridge of his nose. I, on the other hand, had a mop of curly brown hair and green eyes, like my father. Brian was a year older than me, but despite our obvious differences, people often mistook us for twins.

Brian and I were the only two people on earth who knew the extent of what was happening in our home. We carried secrets and shame that only we could understand. We attended every school together, experienced every adventure together, and carried our little suitcases to new homes together, side by side.

When I was in the first grade, we lived in an apartment that was just down the street from our elementary school. The kitchen had fake wood paneled cabinets and yellowed linoleum floors, the kind that always looked dirty no matter how often you scrubbed them. Our mismatched furniture had survived more moves than I could count, sagging and scuffed, but still somehow holding together.

Upstairs, there were two bedrooms with one full bathroom between them. The beige carpet was rough under bare feet, forever dotted with stains and singed in tiny patches from my brother's pyrotechnic experiments. Brian liked to set cotton balls on fire with matches and let them burn out on the floor, leaving little black fingerprints of destruction. I can still see my mother on her hands and knees, scissors in hand, snipping out the charred bits of carpet in a desperate plea to save her security deposit.

Brian and I found a kitten once, shivering in the bushes right outside our front door. He was the tiniest ball of stringy white fur with bright blue eyes, and was so small, even in our six- and seven-year-old

hands. It seemed impossible that he would survive without our intervention. So we decided to save him by smuggling him inside. We hid
"Snowball," the obvious name, in our bedroom closet for almost a week.

We thought that we could somehow keep this tiny, helpless creature
a secret. Maybe we could have if we knew anything about raising a kitten.
We didn't have a litter box or cat food, just that dark closet and some
whole milk stolen from the fridge downstairs.

Did you know that kittens can't drink cow's milk? Their little
stomachs can't handle it.

Poor Snowball pooped *everywhere*. It was hopelessly soaked into
the rug, and everything else on the floor of that closet. Our laundry and
shoes were covered. Between the clothes and the smell he wasn't a secret
for very long and that stench haunted the closet (the entire upstairs,
really) until the day we moved out.

It was in this apartment where I learned to negotiate my own punishment.

I don't even remember what stupid thing I did wrong, but it literally could have been anything. This particular day though my mother
must have been feeling generous. In what I can only assume was meant
to be compassion, she let me choose my fate.

Imagine a six-year-old negotiating the terms of her own punishment,
like I had any real power in that moment.

I had two choices:

A) No treat from the ice cream man.

B) A spanking with a wooden spoon, followed by a "Big Stick" from
the ice cream man.

Now, you need to understand something: we never had treats. Not
real ones, anyway. No cookies in the cupboard, no candy stashed away,
no sodas in the fridge. Sugar was a luxury we couldn't afford, or maybe
one my mother just wouldn't allow. I remember sneaking spoonfuls of
sugar straight from the bowl because it was the sweetest thing in the
house. And later, when my mother would notice sugar spilled on the
counter, even that earned me a spanking.

So when the ice cream man's tinny music echoed through the
parking lot of the apartment complex, it was an event. A Big Stick—that
red-and-orange popsicle for just twenty-five cents—was as close to magic

as my life got. Cold, sweet, sticky summer in your hand. It was the only time I tasted something that felt like childhood was supposed to feel.

Of course, I chose the Big Stick.

The spanking was painful, just like any other, but at least that time I had a reward coming. Once that popsicle touched my tongue, it was absolutely worth it.

It was fucking delicious.

And honestly? I would take a spanking today for a Big Stick.

We had a corporal punishment system in our family. If we broke the rules, we were punished. But the punishment was not graded to match the severity of the offense. The whole system was inconsistent. It was a little too willy-nilly for my liking.

For example:

Eat sugar from the sugar bowl → belt or wooden spoon.

Come home late from school → spoon or ping-pong paddle.

Tell a lie → matchbox racetrack, belt, or spoon.

Set the rug on fire → belt, or honestly, whatever was in reach.

And the swats made no sense either. Sometimes it was five. Sometimes twenty. We never knew.

Kids need structure, you know?

Anyway, given the randomness of it all and the fact that we could be hit at any time for any infraction, Brian and I lived in a constant state of hyper-vigilance. Which, from what I hear, is a perfectly healthy way to be raised.

Based on the frequency and intensity of those punishments, you'd think I was a hardened criminal by the age of six. But no. I was just a typical little girl; shy around strangers, desperate for a Cabbage Patch Doll, loved climbing trees, any apartment complex that had a pool, and I adored my grandparents.

I was just a regular kid.

As an adult, I've never felt the urge to get in touch with that inner child.

The thought of it makes me cringe a little bit. Because, as fun as an apartment complex swimming pool could be, I also grew up knowing my own father couldn't be bothered to stay long enough to hold me, and that, based on how my mother treated me, I must have been completely unlovable.

With that knowledge settled in my heart, my inner child has spent the better part of forty years curled up in a corner, sucking her thumb, too afraid to stand on her own two feet and march out into the world.

Visiting that child stirs up so many memories. There are cardboard boxes in my attic filled with photographs from a childhood I'd rather not revisit. Every picture is a key to a room I've been avoiding for years.

There is a picture of me with an apartment kitchen in the background—orange Formica countertop, cheap dark cabinets, tacky furniture. Every texture unsettles me. Not just because it was the '80s and everything was hideous, but because I remember the room in my bones.

In another photo I'm wearing a strawberry dress and patent leather Mary Janes. The marbled carpet where I sit reminds me of every apartment we had ever lived in. Having a single mother in Southern California meant we were struggling, which meant we moved. A lot. I changed schools at least once every year. Eight times in third grade alone. The picture of me in the strawberry dress makes me feel lonely.

The Disneyland photo is different. That night, when we walked out of a shop on Main Street, my family turned left, and I went right. I'm sure I was terrified when I realized I was alone in a sea of people at the happiest place on earth. But the feeling I get from that picture isn't fear; it's comfort. I was taken to the lost-and-found hut and given a Mickey Mouse coloring book and a bucket of broken crayons, probably used by every other child who had been separated from their family. When my mother rushed into the security hut, she wore a face I had never seen before but immediately recognized. She was happy to see me, relieved even. That's what I remember most—not being lost, but being found.

Then there is the picture from my freshman year of high school. Boy, what a mess. Wild, wispy curls worn half up and half down, so unruly it looked like I'd been shaken upside down before the picture was taken. I had sunburned cheeks and was wearing a floral jumper I wasn't quite filling out yet, creating awkward points on my chest. It was a vibe, that's for sure.

That picture gives me an anxious jolt right in my gut. That was the year our loosey-goosey punishment system would change our lives in ways we never saw coming.

Every photograph, each tied to a moment in time, was a snapshot of the instability I always lived with. And even though Brian isn't in every photo, he's in every room. He was the one who walked in beside me, sat down next to me, and endured what waited there with me.

If my childhood was a house full of rooms I didn't want to enter, Brian was the only other person who knew the layout by heart.

The Magician

When I was eight, I decided to solve loneliness with magic.

Not metaphorical magic, or the kind that comes from kindness, or confidence, or whatever adults mean when they say, "just be yourself."

No. I mean *actual* magic.

Cards. Coins. Illusions.

The kind of magic that could make loneliness disappear in a puff of milk and newspaper.

I was in the third grade, in *another* new school, and I had no friends. Not one. So naturally, I thought, "You know what kids love? Performance art."

My plan was simple: become so dazzlingly magical that friendship would be unavoidable.

Somehow, I convinced a teacher to let me roam the school with a rolling table and a handful of tricks, and I would perform for the other classes. Like a traveling magician whose main trick was making people uncomfortable.

I even had an assistant: a girl from my class. I don't know if she volunteered or was drafted as a behavioral intervention, but either way, she was stuck with me. Together, we wheeled my table of dreams down the hall like we were headlining the world's saddest Vegas residency.

The tricks were classic: pouring milk into a newspaper and making it "disappear." Making coins vanish and reappear behind someone's ear. Pulling scarves from boxes that were... *plot twist*, never actually empty.

The other kids just stared. Not with awe. Not with delight. But with concern. The kind of look that says, "Is she... okay?"

Once, a girl in the back row smiled. A real smile, like maybe she got it. My heart raced, and I smiled back, hopeful. Then she looked away.

Each time I rolled into a new classroom, I thought, "This is it. This is the one. The trick will work here." Not the milk trick. The *big* trick. The one where I stop being the weird girl with no friends and start being someone worth sitting with at lunch.

Shockingly, that one never landed. Turns out sleight of hand doesn't fix chronic unpopularity.

When the tricks were over, I packed up my little table, coins sticky with milk, and rolled off into the fluorescent sunset. The applause was polite, the pity was palpable... and the loneliness? Still very much present.

Sometimes I think about that poor little magician with her tiny table squeaking down the hall, her pockets full of quarters and hope.

I can't tell her the magic will work. Because it won't. But the show went on anyway. It always does.

Rooms With
Revolving Doors

Considering we moved so often when I was growing up, I was well into adulthood before I could grow roots and find a sense of stability.

There were times when things seemed to be okay. My mother worked as a respiratory therapist in a hospital, often pulling back-to-back shifts to make sure we had a place to live and food on the table. Southern California is an expensive place to live, and as a single mother with no child support to speak of, it was all on her to provide for us. I remember her working a lot of double shifts so she could put a few presents under the tree at Christmas.

She was only nineteen when she had Brian, and twenty-one when she started raising me. While I don't think anyone is ever really ready to become a parent, my mother was the kind of person who thought she knew everything, and wasn't interested in learning that she didn't. She was figuring things out as she went, but not really growing from her mistakes.

Even with all her "wisdom," every few months, she would hit her breaking point.

Brian and I were fluent in tension; we could always sense the shift happening in our mother.

Following a spell of frequent double shifts, we would see her patience wear thin. She would start nitpicking everything we did: our chores weren't completed to her liking, our homework wasn't done on time, someone left an apple core behind the ficus in the living room... okay, that gripe was fair, and it was me. I will finally admit that I left the eaten apple core behind the ficus in the living room. We were punished with slaps across the butt or hand for smaller infractions, and a belt, wooden spoon, or occasional ping-pong paddle for something more significant. As Brian and I felt the tension and punishments rising, we knew that we had overstayed our welcome.

When our mother finally had enough, she would open her address book and find a bridge that hadn't yet been burned. She was looking for a relative who would take her children in because she just could not do it anymore.

We were handed off to every family member who would open their doors to us: my grandparents, my uncle, my aunt, my great aunt, and even a grandfather we'd never met before. At just five and six years old, we spent a summer with distant relatives in Oklahoma whom we had never even met before they picked us up from the airport. And so it went, from one place to another, never sure how long we would be there.

Each move was like an earthquake. Sometimes the shift was small, sometimes it was catastrophic. Either way, I could never seem to get my footing. I was always waiting for the sound of my mother's car pulling into an unfamiliar driveway. I lived always half-packed, always ready. The smell of someone else's laundry detergent on sheets that weren't mine. The weight of a suitcase in my small hands.

Every new family meant enrolling in a new school. New teachers, new kids, new insecurities. Starting over somewhere new is scary, and we were scared a lot. Sometimes I would get lucky and make a friend whom I would inevitably have to say goodbye to only a few months later. Every goodbye splintering something inside me, leaving hairline cracks filled with loneliness, cracks that no one could see but that I could always feel.

Some of the homes we moved into were everything I ever wanted. A beautiful room of my own with a pink comforter and a white wrought-iron bed. Wood floors with a round woven rug. Dogs and backyards.

In those homes, we had delicious meals, not the tuna noodle casserole or something resembling goulash that my mother made. We sat together around a dining room table. There were doilies, books, and games. There was laughter and long talks about whatever I wanted to talk about.

I have always had so much to say. And there was something so comforting about having somebody there to listen.

Then there were the other houses, like the house of my maternal grandfather Greg. Until the summer we were sent to live with him, Brian and I had never even met Greg. He was my mother's father, a man who had left his own children with physical and emotional scars that we didn't yet understand. He was such a problematic figure that none of his own children attended his funeral.

What a charmer, huh?

Greg was the kind of man who cast a long shadow over everyone around him. His wife, Sharon, was no different. To me, she looked exactly like a witch. Very thin, slightly hunched, with long dark hair draped over her sharp shoulders. Her nose curved into a hook. Everything about her seemed pointy, as though she had been carved out of angles.

That house felt like it was pulled straight from a nightmare. It was all about discipline. We did what we were told, when we were told, and if we stepped out of line, the punishment came swiftly. Most often, it was lectures.

They were long, punishing stretches of words that could last for hours. Brian and I would sit on the lumpy brown-and-gold couch, its fabric covered in tacky flowered print that was scratchy on the back of our legs, while Greg and Sharon circled us with disappointment. Each word felt heavy, echoing through that room until the air itself seemed thick with failure.

That room is still sealed in my memory, dim and airless, haunted by their voices. Thankfully, the lectures were the extent of the punishments for me. My brother got it a lot worse. Have you ever had to pick your own switch?

When Brian screwed up in a way Greg thought required more than a lecture, he would send him outside to "pick a switch." Brian had to walk out to the yard and choose a branch from a tree, knowing full well he was about to hand over the very thing Greg would use to beat him.

He had to carefully weigh his options. Too thin, and it breaks the skin. Too thick, and it feels like you're being hit with a bat. Either way, pain is coming.

He was only nine years old.

We found out years later that Greg had abused all of his children, including our mother. So, while he was an absolute garbage human, I'm grateful he never turned that violence on me. And maybe, somewhere in all of this, there's a room in that house where my mother is still a hurt child.

Not that it erases what she did to us. But, my heart breaks for everyone he hurt: my mother, my brother, my uncles, all of them. Watching Brian endure that kind of abuse is something I will never forget.

Despite all the instability—or maybe because of it—we usually did well in our new homes. I excelled in school, and Brian was very charming. We were both smart kids, and when given love and structure, we thrived. But that was something my mother couldn't stand.

It seemed that she saw our success as a challenge. Nobody would raise her children better than she could. As soon as she heard we were happy and settled, she would appear at the door, ready to reclaim us. She would tell Brian and I to pack our things as we were heading back "home" again.

Wherever that happened to be.

Back with my mother, the story was always the same. She never said she missed us or that she couldn't live without us. Instead, she would tell us we caused too many problems, that they didn't want us anymore, that we embarrassed her.

We were always the problem.

The message was clear: we were not cherished. She did not fight for us. We were a nuisance, an inconvenience to everyone—including our own mother. All that moving, all that being shifted around, carved a belief into me: that I was tolerated, not accepted. That roots, for me at least, were impossible.

When you grow up in that environment, you start to believe you don't deserve to belong anywhere. You learn to read a room before you enter it, to measure your worth by how little space you take up, to pack light because heavy things are harder to carry when you're asked to leave.

That belief followed me into every room of my life. Even when a door was wide open, I never felt sure I was allowed to stay. I would stand at thresholds, one foot in, one foot out, always prepared for the inevitable moment when I would hear: pack your things, it's time to go.

Still, for all the instability and the constant stress, I've learned to find a strange sort of strength in it. I can walk into any room and make myself at home. I can make a friend anywhere, and sense when someone else needs one, too.

I'm not grateful for the insecurity it left me with, or for the chronic need to please people just to keep the peace. But I can see the lesson in it. The rooms that weren't mine taught me how to read the temperature of a space, how to listen for safety, and how to create comfort even when it isn't offered.

Those temporary houses and the abandonment that shaped me also gave me something unexpected: the ability to build belonging wherever I go.

The Room with Chives

N ot every home we were sent to felt like exile. Some, it turned out, felt like safety. The trick was learning to believe I was allowed to stay there.

My grandparents' condo in Los Angeles felt like a palace compared to the apartments Brian and I were used to. Four levels, with carpeted stairs that seemed to go on forever, and a game closet that was pure magic. We would pull out Monopoly or Bingo, spreading the pieces across the floor while the afternoon sun slanted through the windows.

My grandpa taught me how to outline pictures in a coloring book before filling them in, so the color wouldn't bleed over the lines. He made me believe I could make anything neater and prettier, more controlled than the mess life handed me. My grandma made us buckwheat pancakes, my favorite, and would take us shopping for new clothes.

Their place was immaculate and decorated so nicely. There was never any clutter. The cream-colored carpet always had lines like it had just been freshly vacuumed. My grandmother ironed everything: their jeans, sweatshirts, and even the sheets for the bed.

My grandpa washed his own towels separately from my grandmother's laundry because he wanted a fresh towel for every shower. He told us he did this because "no matter how careful you are, if you use the same towel twice, there is a chance you will wipe your face with your own ass."

We'd laugh, and for those weekends, everything felt almost normal. Like we were just regular kids with regular grandparents who told silly jokes and made pancakes.

One morning, when we were spending the weekend with them, Grandma had made my favorite pancakes. While we ate, I accidentally knocked over my glass of milk. The sound of it hitting the table sent a jolt of pure terror through my body. I panicked and cried, trying to clean it up as quickly as possible, my hands shaking as I grabbed for napkins. In my head, I was already calculating the punishment, already bracing for the anger. That kind of survival instinct isn't natural in a seven-year-old girl.

But my grandmother, in her perfectly pressed pajamas and robe, gently took the napkins from my hands, and as she blotted the milk off the table, she smiled at me and said, "April, honey, there is no need to cry over spilled milk."

The reaction from my grandma was normal; mine was not. I was a product of my environment. As safe as I felt with my grandparents, the trauma from home was always lingering just under the fragile surface. Looking back at these moments, I can see the distance between the child I was and the child I might have been. In that gap lived all the rooms I had survived, all the ways I had learned to anticipate disaster, all the reasons I couldn't simply enjoy a stack of pancakes without fear.

My grandpa loved his cars. Still does. He polished them so clean you could see your reflection in the paint. Every time we went into the garage, he'd shake his finger at us and say, "You touch my car, I'll break your fingers." We always laughed, but it was a nervous laugh, the kind of laugh only kids who'd seen too much violence could make.

We never touched Grandpa's cars.

There was a pool in the condo complex, and in those summers, it became our world. Brian and I splashed and swam while Grandma and Grandpa stretched out on lounge chairs, sunglasses on, soaking up the California sun. My grandparents were young—she was only thirty-four years old when Brian was born, and Grandpa wasn't much older.

For once, I felt safe. Safe in my body, safe in my family, safe in the water.

Until the day Brian ruined it for everybody.

Brian pooped in the community pool.

Can you even?

And not just any poop... a huge floater. My grandmother was mortified. They had to drain the pool, disinfect it, the whole nine yards.

We were blacklisted from the pool for the rest of the season. Even now, decades later, the memory makes me both cringe and laugh.

My grandparents were, and still are, my safe space. They've been the steady room in my house of memories for my entire life. When I think of them, I think of structural integrity in its purest form; the quiet, dependable kind that doesn't draw attention to itself but keeps everything standing.

They didn't need to fix what was broken; they just stayed steady enough for me to feel okay. They didn't ask me to be anything other than what I was. They didn't require me to earn my place at their table. In their home, I knew love was as simple as buckwheat pancakes and a gentle voice saying, "There's no need to cry."

Even at forty-five years old, when I brought my husband and daughter to stay with them in their new home in Nevada, it still felt like coming home. The space itself was different; no longer in Los Angeles. The new space in Nevada was two bedrooms, one level, still organized and spotless. The energy was the same. The love, the feeling of warmth and acceptance, still filled the air.

There's one thing of theirs that has been mine in spirit forever: a light brown stuffed bear named Chives. He's bigger than your average bear, measuring approximately three feet tall, almost fifty years old, a little scratchy, and the handsomest bear there ever was.

Somewhere in my attic is a picture of me as a toddler, fast asleep on Chives like he was the world's greatest pillow. The last time we visited my grandparents, Grandma told me that after a lifetime with her, she wanted Chives to have a new home with me.

What an absolute honor.

We couldn't carry Chives on the plane, so we headed to UPS to ship him to his new home in New York. As the clerk slid him gently into a box, she smiled and said, "Okay, Mr. Bear, in you go."

I corrected her immediately: "Ma'am, his name is Chives."

Mr. Bear. How ridiculous.

Chives isn't just a bear; he's a doorway. One hug and I'm back in that condo, with sun-warmed skin and pancakes on the table. A room I can always step into, one that never stops being mine. This is what I learned from my grandparents: that some rooms don't lock their doors behind you. Some rooms stay open, waiting for you to return, no matter how long you've been gone.

Now Chives lives in my walk-in closet, perched on a dresser. At least once a week, I give him, yes, a bear hug and bury my face in his fur. He smells like my grandparents, like the best parts of my childhood, like safety. If the rest of my childhood was filled with stress and instability, Chives is the artifact that proves some rooms were built strong enough to last.

The Room with
The Broken Glass

When I was eleven and Brian was twelve, my mother met a man in a bar. They got married within the year, and when I was thirteen, my younger brother was born. For the seven years until I moved out of the house, there was a kind of stability we had never experienced before.

At least, it looked that way from the outside.

Inside the house, though, my stepdad struggled with alcoholism, which, as it usually does, affected the entire family. Some days, he would drink a six-pack of Coors Light and be funny. "Are you a fart smeller or a smart feller?" he would ask, laughing at his own joke with a loud, gulping kind of laugh.

Those nights, we could breathe.

Other nights, he would lose his temper over seemingly nothing. On those nights, we held our breath.

My mother never drank, thankfully, but when he would lose control, they would fight, screaming at each other in the living room of our 1,200-square-foot house. We could hear everything from our bedrooms down the hall. He would punch walls, throw lamps, and stomp around like he was a big man.

It's a small consolation that at least he never hit any of us.

Occasionally, he would be an angry drunk too often. This would push my mother over her threshold for bullshit. She would tell us to pack our stuff, and we would all leave. My mother, Brian, Chris and I would move into an apartment, leaving my stepdad alone in the house.

Months would go by, and he would finally apologize. He would swear that he would stop drinking, and make promises to attend church on Sundays. It was always the promise of church that did the trick for my mom. We would pack up the apartment and move back home.

Church was my mother's love language. When he promised to go, she heard repentance. She heard change. She believed that if he could just sit in those pews, God would fix what she couldn't. Therefore, every promise to attend Sunday service became proof that this time would be different.

However, he was still an alcoholic, so it wasn't long before he would have "just one beer," and the cycle would continue. We lived in an endless loop.

One particular night, I woke to the familiar sound of slurred anger. On nights like that, I would lie still in bed, afraid to breathe. Even with my door closed, I did not want to draw any attention to myself. The instability in the air was terrifying.

As the yelling escalated, I heard the crashing of glass. Holding my breath, I calculated how far away it sounded, trying to decipher what had been broken. It sounded like something smaller, maybe a drinking glass? They both continued yelling, which meant no one was hurt.

The shouting came closer, and closer, until suddenly my bedroom door flew open. I shot straight up in my bed, breath caught in my throat as my mother yelled frantically. "Pack a bag! We can't stay here!" She ran to my brother's room next and repeated the command.

I knew the drill. I threw on a sweatshirt over my pajamas, grabbed my backpack, and stuffed in a few pairs of socks and underwear, some clothes for the next couple of days, then scrambled into the bathroom for my toothbrush, hairbrush, and a scrunchie.

Brian and I packed in silence, our hands moving fast from muscle memory. I was scared, but I had done this so many times that my hands moved on autopilot, my fear locked deep inside.

When we were each packed up, my mother ordered us to the car. She didn't follow right away, so Brian and I sat in the cold back seat, breath fogging the air, waiting silently. Finally, my mother appeared in the doorway, my stepfather looming behind her with his arms raised as he shouted threats. She slammed the door behind her and ran toward the car.

My mom opened the back door to toss in her overnight bag, and then she saw it.

A wrench.

Time stopped.

This wasn't any wrench. This was a heavy-duty pipe wrench. It was over two feet long and looked as though it weighed around fifteen pounds. I saw the change in my mother's face: from fear to determination.

She slowly reached down, wrapped her fingers around the handle, and lifted it toward her body. As she began walking away with it, the next few seconds played out in my mind like a horror film.

Until that moment, I had been numb, almost detached from what was happening that night. On autopilot. Survival mode. But when she picked up that wrench, something inside me broke open.

She was going to march over to my stepdad's beloved truck and smash the windows, the windshield, the doors. He would explode, run toward her, rip the wrench from her hands, and in a blind, drunken rage, turn it on her. I would sit helplessly in the car as my mother was beaten in front of me.

I scrambled toward her, crying so hard I could barely speak, my voice cracking into something I didn't recognize.

"Mom. Please. Don't do it. Please. Let's just go. Please. Mom, he's coming."

Thank God for the divine intervention that led her to hear me. She paused, put the wrench back on the floor under my feet, jumped into the driver's seat, and drove us away.

Every time we packed up and returned, I would tell myself maybe this time it would last. Maybe he really had changed. But addiction doesn't make for good structure. You can't rebuild a home on a foundation of empty Coors Light cans and broken promises.

The Room That
Left a Mark

For the first time in my life, I had real friends. The kind I'd always imagined having.

We talked on the phone for hours. Had sleepovers on the weekends. Rode our bikes all over the neighborhood. Once, we even made a pie filled with dog shit to get back at a neighborhood bully. It felt like something out of a TV montage, the best group of friends.

And then high school came.

Brian went to Westminster High first, as he was a year ahead of me. He got into a lot of fights that year, so our mother decided the school was violent and therefore unsafe. The irony: our home was also violent and unsafe.

She transferred us to another district.

I started my freshman year at Fountain Valley High School, while all of the friends I had made went to Westminster.

I was devastated.

I was fourteen, starting over again. Most of the kids at this new school had known each other their whole lives. I knew no one.

Where would I find my place?

I enrolled in theatre classes my freshman year and loved it. You know how theatre kids are, right? They love to collect strays. And that's exactly what I was. A stray looking for a room to belong in.

Some of my favorite high school memories happened in that theatre room. The walls were painted black, the chairs stacked on risers facing the stage with the light booth glowing behind us. In that space, we were free to play pretend. I pretended to be in a Phil Collins music video, yes, the one with the drum riff. I played parts from *The Miracle Worker*, *The Glass Menagerie*, *The Odd Couple*, and *The Diary of Anne Frank*.

We all grew up in that room. We fell in love, we laughed, we cried. We shared everything. Maybe we were supposed to be learning about acting, but what we were really learning was how to be ourselves. That theatre room was the first space that didn't ask me to shrink or toughen up. It just held me. For once, the walls around me felt safe enough to lean on.

I also played the flute in the marching band, briefly, a carryover from middle school. I loved that instrument. I would sit in my bedroom with books of sheet music my mother found for me, and I would play for hours, losing myself in the sound. The flute felt like an escape from my house, a doorway into another world where no one could touch me.

My new school, being a town away, was far. Like three and a half miles each way, far. Brian and I had to get to and from school, on bike or on foot, rain or shine, uphill both ways... you know how it goes. It's worth noting that we were required to be home from school thirty minutes after the final class ended. No fraternizing, no loitering, just getting our asses home.

If we didn't make it back on time, we risked punishment: anything from three swats with the hand to no TV for a week to a ruthless beating. Who knew? It was a game of Russian roulette we didn't want to play. Ever.

Can we just talk about that time restriction for a second? Three and a half miles in thirty minutes. Twice a day. With a full backpack, a flute, and a lunch box, in Payless sneakers.

It wasn't discipline. It was punishment disguised as cardio.

Every day was a race against the clock. Every day, the anxiety bubbled in my stomach.

What if I was late?

What if the bike got a flat?

What if, what if, what if.

One day during my freshman year, for whatever reason, Brian didn't bring his bike to school, but I did. We agreed that he would ride my bike home, and I would sit on the handlebars so we could both get home within the thirty minutes we were allotted.

Minutes later, I was sitting on the handlebars of my own bike, holding on for dear life while Brian pedaled us home. We were cruising along and making good time as we approached the first freeway overpass on our route. It was a steep climb and, with two people, two backpacks, two lunch boxes, and a flute, Brian really had to work to get us up that hill.

The other side of the hill was the reward for the climb. If you pedaled quickly enough, you could coast at a good speed for at least a couple of blocks while giving your legs a much-needed rest.

And that's what he did. He picked up as much speed as he could coming over the top of the hill so we could coast as long as possible. We were flying. I picked an unfortunate time to adjust my butt on the handlebars, pushing my cheap sneakers into the one-inch bolts on each side of the front wheel while holding on for dear life.

As I shifted my weight forward, we hit a dip in a driveway. The handlebars jerked. My feet slipped. The wind rushed past my ears. At that speed, traveling downhill with all that weight in those crappy Payless shoes...

There was absolutely nothing I could do.

Isn't it funny how instability always announces itself after the fall? One second you're flying high; the next, you're sifting through the rubble to see what's left.

When I opened my eyes, an officer was sitting next to me, looking so calm that I wasn't sure what had happened. My ears were ringing. His mouth was moving, but I couldn't hear the words. The sky was bright and perfectly blue.

Wait. Why was I on the ground?

And then the pain hit me: What the... FUCK, my face hurt.

Where the hell did this cop even come from? How long had I been sitting there?

An ambulance arrived and I was loaded in and taken to the hospital. Brian and my bike were in the cruiser following close behind.

Oh, my poor face. I'd hit the pavement face-first, with my right hand the only backup to take the force. I had small fractures in my nose and wrist plus the fattest, bloodiest lips I'd ever seen outside of a boxing match.

Brian swears he didn't run me over, and I have no way to prove that he did. But does anyone honestly believe he didn't at least clip me? I do not. I am fully convinced that, adding insult to very literal injury, he ran me over with my own bike while I was lying face-down on the pavement like a human speed bump.

Did I mention I was a freshman in a new school?

I had to go back a few days later, my taco-meat-looking face held high. But thankfully, even high schoolers knew enough to be kind.

Because of my wrist injury, I had to quit marching band. Which was fine, I still had the theatre. But it was more change, and I spent quite a few nights crying about it. Or more likely, I was just crying about my face.

Over time, though, my face healed. I had my people in theatre. I was even happy to go to school every day. For a little while, I forgot that happiness in my house was always temporary.

The Room Behind
the Velvet Rope

My baby brother Chris was my entire world. I took him everywhere with me, like he was my own baby. Our mother worked nights and slept during the day, and my stepdad worked long days as a crane operator. If I wasn't at school, I was taking care of Chris.

He was the best thing that had ever happened to me. I loved Chris so much that I'd sneak into his room while he slept and lie on the floor, just to be near him.

He adored me, too. He lit up when I came home from school, he laughed at all my peek-a-boos and fake sneezes and squealed every time I would throw him up into the air and catch him.

But even though I loved him fiercely, I couldn't help noticing how different things were for him than they had been for me.

Growing up, I wanted to be in gymnastics and Girl Scouts. I wanted to run track in high school. I wanted to belong to something where kids wore sashes or uniforms, where moms cheered or clapped or pinned badges onto fabric. But the answer was always no.

No money. No time.

Just no.

Except when it came to Chris.

Chris was in Little League. Not just Little League, though; he was on travel teams, had the nicest new equipment, and private pitching lessons from a retired professional ball player. He had uniforms, cleats, gear bags, and a mom who sat in the bleachers keeping score and handing out orange slices. She was the team mom; the kind of mom I always wanted her to be.

She was all of that for *him*.

Chris was good at it, too. He had a natural swing and loved the game in a way that was genuine. It wasn't his fault that he was chosen.

But the difference in treatment was glaring. Chris was our stepdad's child, and Brian and I were not.

Looking back now, I can understand the math of it: spending his money on his child was safe. Spending it on Brian or me could feel risky. Maybe, in my mother's mind, it would jeopardize the safety net she had built for herself. Maybe she believed that his love had limits, that his money had strings, and that our best chance at any stability was keeping him happy.

But as a child, I did not have that perspective. I didn't see generational trauma, or scarcity mindsets, or a woman clawing her way toward survival. What I saw was a mother putting her energy into one child while her other children learned to live without.

And when you're a child, you don't translate neglect as "my parent is broken." You translate it as "I am not enough."

I can still picture myself at the kitchen table, filling out the registration form for a community gymnastics program I would never get to hand in. The pen felt heavy in my hand, and a twinge of hope bubbled up in my heart.

A few of my friends were in it. I saw their T-shirts, listened to them talk about their routines, and sat quietly on the sidelines of their excitement. I didn't want medals or trophies. I just wanted to be part of the conversation.

I just wanted to belong.

She didn't even glance at the form. "We don't have the money for that," she said, and went back to stirring something on the stove. The smell of dinner cooking. The sound of the spoon scraping the pot.

Meanwhile, Chris was at practice.

I always seemed to be grounded. Once, I was grounded for an entire month because while Brian and I had been arguing, I wrote "Fuck you, Brian" on a piece of loose-leaf paper, folded it into a paper airplane, and threw it across the room at him. We both forgot about it, and my mother found it behind the couch days later. She recognized my handwriting, and that was it. One month: no television, no phone, no friends. Over a few words on a piece of paper.

Yet Chris could leave his baseball gear scattered across the living room or backtalk, and he'd get nothing more than a gentle reminder about his behavior.

It wasn't discipline. It was containment. Restrictions that kept me and my life small. And because there was no way to win, no way to fight back, I started to believe the punishments weren't about me at all. They made life easier for her.

If I was grounded, I wouldn't be asking for rides to go to the skating rink with my best friend, Stacey. I wouldn't be asking for a few dollars for pizza night with my friends or begging to stay on the phone in the kitchen, stretching the cord as far as it would go, just for a little privacy.

I was out of the way. And maybe that was the point.

Being a stepchild meant being in the room, but not part of it. There was this invisible velvet rope, and I was always on the wrong side of it.

Understanding how trauma shapes us cuts both ways. Now, as an adult, I can see my mother as a scared woman doing what she thought she had to do to maintain this security. At the same time, I see myself as a scared little girl who learned that being small meant being safe.

While forgiveness doesn't come easily to me, I have spent years working on forgiving myself for trying to earn a love that should have been freely given. And maybe, on my best days, I can even forgive her. Because just as I did what I thought was necessary for my survival, she did too.

Being a stepchild taught me how to survive without being chosen. How to keep going even when you're overlooked. How to build a family later in life where my daughter will never wonder if she's on the wrong side of the velvet rope.

It's a wound, yes. But it's also what made me fight to create something different. And standing here now, years away from that kitchen table and that gymnastics form I never got to hand in, I can finally say I was always enough.

Even when they never saw me.

The Room with
The Palm Tree

Not everything in that house was a nightmare. We had "normal" family moments, too.

We had a big yellow boat named "Fresh One" that was trailered in our driveway. We used to sit on the Tuna tower of that boat and would watch the Disneyland fireworks over the trees. We went camping by a lake, and I learned to water ski behind a friend's boat. We spent a lot of days at Huntington Beach, either boogie boarding or fishing from the pier.

But even in the lighter moments, there was always something lurking underneath. My stepdad's drinking meant that any sense of stability was temporary; we never knew if we were walking into laughter or into a storm. That uncertainty lived under everything. Even during the holidays.

One Christmas, our entire world almost collapsed, and it had nothing to do with Coors Lite.

It was a couple of days before Christmas, and we had all been shopping at the mall. This was the '90s and mall shopping was an event. We sampled perfumes in the department store, trying to match the right scent to the right relative. We stopped at Sharper Image to find the newest cool gadget, and we always bought a little gift box of cured meats from Hickory Farms.

We stopped by the Christmas tree lot on our way home and picked up our family tree. We came home happy, arms full of bags and holiday cheer. For once, everything felt normal. Safe, even.

That night after we brought the tree home, my stepdad trimmed it right there in the living room to save himself the hassle of dragging the tree outside to trim it, and back in again. Nobody thought this would be a big deal; it just meant there would be pine needles all over the carpet, only a little extra cleanup.

My brother, Brian, was diagnosed with asthma when he was very little. As kids, we spent so many nights in emergency rooms while he received breathing treatments and steroids to help him breathe. I would sit on cold, hard hospital chairs at 3 or 4 o'clock in the morning, reading whatever book I had borrowed from the school library. One summer, I read Charlie and the Chocolate Factory by Roald Dahl three times over several ER visits, waiting for my brother to be discharged.

The day we spent Christmas shopping, Brian had been complaining all day. So, as he sat whining about having to help with the tree, our mother had enough and sent him to bed.

Brian came out of his room a few minutes later, complaining that he was having trouble breathing. As this was fairly common, my mother had a plan in place. We had a nebulizer and medication for him at home now, so we weren't running to the hospital every time the inhaler failed to help him.

Brian sat in the bathroom, on the closed toilet lid, steam pumping from the nebulizer. He sucked in the medicine as best he could, but he wasn't getting better. He looked tense, but weak, trying like hell to get some air. His lips started turning blue. All of a sudden, I watched my brother slump over, falling toward the sink. He was fading fast.

My mom yelled for me to go into my room, close the door, and not come out. The look in her eyes let me know this was not a suggestion. I closed my door and then sat on the other side with my shoulder and ear pressed against it. I held my breath to hear everything that was happening just a few feet away. My heart pounded so hard I was afraid they could hear it.

Please. Please. Please God help my brother. I didn't know what else to do, so I prayed over and over again.

Our mother was a respiratory therapist. She taught CPR classes at the local hospital for extra money. But when she cried out to my stepdad to call 911, she asked for directions on how to perform CPR. In her panic, she had forgotten something she had taught to hundreds of other people.

My stepdad shouted instructions from the kitchen. "Give him a breath, and then pump his chest fifteen times... okay, now give him another breath!"

I don't remember how long it was before I saw the red and blue lights flickering through my bedroom window, and heard the paramedics rush into the house. The memory plays both in fast-forward and slow motion. They intubated Brian, got him oxygen, and rushed him to the hospital.

My mother rode in the ambulance with Brian, and we followed behind, my stepdad driving. I sat in the backseat of the dark blue Ford F250, gripping my own hands and staring out the window at the ambulance, praying my brother was still alive.

Thank God the doctors saved him. Brian spent four days in the hospital, including Christmas Day. I slept on the floor of my mom's room while he was gone as I couldn't be alone. I kept replaying those blue lips and flashing lights. Even after he came home safe, I couldn't shake what I'd almost lost: my brother, my best friend, the only person who knew everything.

When Brian finally came home, I hovered like a shadow. I slept lighter, listened harder, always half-prepared for sirens or chest compressions to become part of our night. That day left a scar in my memory. Not just because of what almost happened, but because it shattered the illusion that we were finally safe.

It was years before we had a real Christmas tree again. I think the avoidance of pine needles and the smell of sap spoke to our shared trauma from that night. Instead, we decorated a fake palm tree that sat in a mauve pot in the corner of our living room. We strung it with beads, candy canes, and colored lights: our strange stand-in for the holiday tradition.

Looking back now, the palm tree feels like both a survival tactic and a memorial, a way of keeping the memory close without inviting it to haunt us every December.

The Tryout

I would like to start by telling you that I am not an athlete. I once had fluid drained from my knee after injuring it while playing ultimate frisbee at the beach. In my defense, I was trying to impress a boy.

I was fast in high school, though. I probably could've run track if I had permission or support. But I didn't.

Maybe in another lifetime.

Knowing these things about myself, I still tried out for the softball team the summer between my sophomore and junior years.

My stomach was in knots the whole drive there. My palms were sweating before I even got out of the car. I was so nervous.

But I was also brave. Not on the field, though. On the field, I was afraid of the ball.

But I was brave enough to show up.

I dragged my poor friend, Stacey, with me. Stacey was decent; she could catch and even throw a little. And at least she could make eye contact with the ball. I couldn't do any of those things.

But that's not even the part that makes me cringe when I think about that day.

Our school's softball team was California State Champions. These girls were *actual* athletes. I bet in their free time they practiced sliding into bases just for fun. They were not looking for, nor did they need, the likes of us.

To this day, I'm convinced they still laugh about the live-action "Who's on First?" routine we performed for them that day.

If my lack of skill didn't get them, my fashion choice certainly did.

All the other girls showed up in real athletic clothes. Coordinated pieces that matched and stretched, tank tops and fitted shorts, sneakers with actual tread.

Me? I showed up in cheap Payless shoes and my gym clothes. Not "clothes I wore to the gym." These were clothes issued to me by the P.E. department. Blue shorts. Gray t-shirt. "Fountain Valley High School" printed across the front, my name scrawled underneath in permanent marker.

What a dork.

I remember standing in the outfield, praying the ball wouldn't come to me. When it did, I felt my heart drop. I reached up anyway with my hands shaking and missed it by a mile.

Somewhere inside me, underneath all the instability and the moving and the never-quite-fitting-in, there was still a spark of hope that maybe this time would be different. Maybe this magic trick would work.

I think about that girl in her PE-issued clothes sometimes. The one who walked onto that field knowing she didn't belong but hoping she'd find a way. The one who was brave enough to risk humiliation for the chance, however small, of being part of a team.

And in case you are wondering, no, that bravery did not get me onto the softball team. But it got me through a lot of other doors later. It taught me that showing up matters, even when you think you're not enough.

Especially then.

The Room That
Broke Me

I grew up on the edge of a normal life filled with love, acceptance, and comfort. There were the glimpses of joy from my mother, however infrequent. The families that took us in and gave us a structured world and safety, and my grandparents who always felt like home.

I knew what peace could feel like, even if I never got to settle into its warmth for very long.

Our life in Westminster had that same sharp edge of living like a family, but not quite. And as someone who could feel the tension rising in any situation, I should have seen the writing on the wall and laid low for a while but instead, I lived like things were normal for a little too long.

When Chris was little I used to play a game with him where I would stand him up at the arm of the couch, his feet on the cushion, and pull his little legs out from under him so fast that his belly would flop onto the couch. Every time, we'd both laugh like crazy. He'd climb back up, look at me, waiting. And... flop! And we'd laugh again.

One day, I didn't pull fast enough, and his little nose scraped down the arm of the couch. I held him while he cried, comforting him until the bleeding stopped. It absolutely broke my heart. Thankfully, aside from a tiny scratch on his otherwise perfect nose, he was fine.

A few days later, I was in the backyard playing with one of Chris's toys. Do you remember the Fisher-Price Corn Popper toy? You know the one: long handle, plastic bubble at the end with little balls inside. The world's worst depiction of popcorn.

I was throwing the toy in the air and catching it like I was a baton twirler on my way to the Olympics. Only I missed the catch, and it came crashing down onto the cement patio. No worries, I picked it up to continue, as I still had a chance to win silver. But when I accidentally dropped it again, it broke into two pieces: the long handle and the ball.

Eh, who was I kidding? I was never going to make it to Beijing like that. Sure, I was upset that I broke it, but as they say, shit happens.

Later that same week, I came home late from school. Not an hour late, maybe fifteen minutes. It was the amount of time you would barely even notice unless you were watching the clock.

The minute I opened the door to our house, I knew something wasn't right. It was too quiet; the air was still. The kind of stillness that made the hair on the back of my neck stand up.

Then I saw her. My mom. She was waiting for me.

Her eyes met mine, and I froze in my tracks. Have you ever seen rage and nothing in a person all at once? That's what I walked into. And in that instant, I knew. This was going to be one of those days. Whatever was about to happen was going to hurt. And there was nothing I could do to stop it.

She grabbed my arm and pulled me into my room while she yelled about all my recent shortcomings: the scratch on Chris's nose, the broken toy, and now this—this unforgivable, fifteen-minute delay. And then I saw the stick. The same blue stick from earlier in the week, the stick that almost took me to the backyard Olympics.

I didn't have time to move. Didn't have time to brace.

Snap! Snap! Snap!

There was so much noise while she swung that stick, striking my back, my butt, and my legs, cracking that stick across my body.

It continued until she felt like it was enough. There was no rhyme or reason to it; she just stopped, turned and walked out of my room and into Brian's. Everything was so loud. Louder than when I woke up on the side of a highway with a bloody face and a concussion.

The noise sounded like heat.

Does that make sense?

Her yelling, me crying, my heart shattering. It all blended into one unbearable, fiery hum.

And then, silence.

As soon as she crossed the threshold heading toward Brian, my room swallowed me whole. This memory, this room, it doesn't live with the others. It's fractured off and sealed away. In its own universe entirely. I knew Brian was suffering the same fate, but his cries could not reach me. The walls held me in, and all I could hear was the roar of my own anguish, pain, and rage.

I didn't see her again that night.

I don't remember falling asleep. I don't remember anything except the ache in my back and the knowledge that morning would come, and I would have to pretend this never happened.

The next morning, I went to school like everything was fine. It wasn't the first time I had to sit a little crooked in my chair because my ass hurt from whatever bullshit punishment I had earned the day before. But this time was different. This time, someone saw the marks.

I had gym for my first class period, and this particular day we were in the weight room. I loved weightlifting. I was weirdly strong for my size and it made me feel good. If I was strong, I could protect myself.

I sat down at the leg press, my favorite machine, and immediately felt a deep, searing pain shoot through my lower back. I gasped. The cold metal against my shirt. The fluorescent lights overhead. Everything felt too sharp. I stood up to move to another machine, and a friend caught sight of the welts and bruises from the night before.

Horrified, she pulled me aside and asked what had happened. My eyes welled up as I immediately got defensive. But before I could brush her off, she called out to our other friends for backup. I managed to hold them off, saying: "I'm fine, I promise. I'll tell you later." My voice was shaking.

When "later" finally came, I broke down and told them everything. I can still see their faces; fourteen-year-old kids trying desperately to help while their hearts broke for me. I hate those faces. I love how much they wanted to help, but I carried so much shame. If my own mother would do this to me, how could anyone else ever think I was worth anything?

One of these friends was the daughter of a police officer. When she told me I couldn't go home and I needed to tell her father what happened, I was terrified. I wanted to run, but where? I couldn't go home because now there was no way I could make it there on time, and I couldn't take any more bruises on my back.

I couldn't tell the police either. My mom would be so angry. And rightfully so, I thought. What kind of monster turns her own mother in to the police?

What if they arrested her?

What if she went to jail?

What would happen to me?

Or worse: what if the police didn't believe me at all and I had to go home with her that night?

There was no winning. No escape. No happy, safe place for me that night. That was a room that didn't exist for me anymore.

Knowing there was no choice, I went home with my friend to see her father. He was still in uniform when we got to the house, having just finished a shift. As kind as his face was, the gun on his hip was definitely intimidating. My friend rushed me upstairs to her bedroom and left me sitting on the edge of her bed while she hurried downstairs to speak with her father.

The few minutes she was gone felt like hours.

Her room was nice enough. A twin bed that looked like it had been made in a hurry that morning. Closet door open, clothes spilling out. I waited, hands on my knees, breath stuck in my throat, hearing the muffled voices from downstairs, and then footsteps. When her father came in, I sat up taller, correcting my posture, like authority had just entered the room.

Was he judging me? Did he believe his daughter? My thoughts raced and I was crying before I could even stop myself.

My friend had told him everything, and he explained to me that I was going to be safe. That we were going into the precinct to file a report, and how I probably wouldn't be going home for a while. I held my friend's hand tightly as we all walked downstairs, out to her father's car, and he drove us to the police station.

When we arrived, everything felt both too bright and too loud, the kind of loud that hums under your skin.

I waited at a desk with plexiglass around it, with a full view of the precinct. I told a woman police officer the same story I had shared with my friends earlier that day. She was calm and patiently took note of everything I said.

Once the report was complete, she needed to take pictures of my injuries. I was escorted to an interrogation room with grey walls and a metal table with two chairs on either side. I did as I was instructed: lifted my shirt and pulled down my pants to show the welts and bruises covering from my lower back to my thighs while another woman took pictures.

They circled me in silence, with only the clicking of the camera documenting the moment. I stood still, facing a wall, as tears ran down my cheeks.

I returned to the desk where I had given my report, and then I saw them. My mother, followed by Brian, and then my stepdad, with Chris in his arms. They were walking into the station behind a uniformed officer.

My mother's face was tight and pinched, almost unrecognizable. I had never seen her make that face before. I still can't place it. Was it betrayal? Embarrassment? Shame? It sure as hell wasn't sympathy for me.

I wanted to disappear. To sink through the floor. Anything but sit there while they all looked at me.

I had never felt as alone as I did in that crowded precinct. Brian had been with me through everything until that day. Now we were separated, and by so much more than space. It felt like we were on opposite sides of a canyon. Him with our mother, and me, alone.

The look on Brian's face is still burned into my memory. He was scared, sure, but even more so, he was angry. As tears streamed down his cheeks, he yelled across the precinct, "Why did you do this? You're ruining our family!"

His words hit me like a fist.

I wonder if he really meant that, or if he was reacting to a silent pact I had broken. Up until this point, no matter what we endured, we endured it together. Was he mad that I did this alone?

I ruined our family.

I was only fourteen years old.

The Room I
Survived Alone

The police station was so scary. I didn't know what my life was going to look like after that night. I only had the moment I was in, and in that moment, I was alone.

My mother was interviewed, processed, given a court date, then she was released. And my family left.

The bravest thing I had ever done was over. Now it was a matter of logistics.

Where would I go? Who would look after me?

A social worker sat down with the kind, practiced face of someone who had done this countless times, and explained what would happen next: I was going to a "children's home," where I would stay until, hopefully, another family member could take me in.

I convinced myself that by the next morning, my grandparents would pick me up and I would finally be safe. For whatever reason, they didn't come for me. Maybe they didn't even know what had happened.

The social worker and I arrived at the children's home in a complex somewhere in Orange County close to midnight. I was led to an office where I was checked in, and it reminded me of every school I'd ever attended: tan metal desks and file cabinets over a tough institutional carpet. Everything felt familiar but also foreign, like a dream that tilted toward a nightmare.

I sat in hard plastic chairs, just like those nights with my brother in the hospital, only he wasn't there. He was home in his room, in his own bed. A tear fell down my cheek.

"You're ruining our family!" echoed in my head.

I spent a couple of hours watching people fill out papers and speak in quiet voices about courts and counseling and lawyers. After an overwhelming flood of information I couldn't possibly absorb, a woman was called to escort me to where I would stay, at least for the night.

I followed this woman down a dark path toward the building where I would finally, *hopefully*, get some rest.

The woman walking with me was quiet. I still think about her sometimes. She was tall and thin, with long, sandy blonde hair. She wasn't dressed in the same business attire as the social worker I had been with earlier; she wore jeans and a white sweatshirt.

What a sad job she had: guiding terrified kids into strange buildings after the unimaginable had happened. Maybe their parents were in prison, or maybe they had died. And there she was, limping alongside me, leading me silently toward another set of strangers.

I've never been the type to let silence just be, especially when I'm nervous. So, halfway down the path, noticing her limp, I casually asked the woman, "What happened to your leg?"

She answered, "Oh, nothing. It's fake."

And here's where I need to defend myself. I was fourteen years old and having the worst day of my life. I was 100% convinced that this woman was telling me that her limp was fake. Like she'd just flat-out admitted: "Yep, totally faking this."

So, I laughed.

I laughed at a woman with what turned out to be a prosthetic leg. She told me her leg was fake, and I laughed at her. Like an absolute monster.

It took me months, long after I'd left that place, to realize what she'd meant. Even now, decades later, I wish I could apologize to her. If she ever sees this, I am so sorry. My laugh was not meant to be cruel. It came from the innocence of a kid who was just trying to survive to the next moment.

A few minutes later, she handed me off to another stranger, and I was shown to a room where I would finally try to sleep. It had to be well after midnight.

Every part of me was exhausted, but fear buzzed through my body like static. I wanted to be back in my room, in our house. Even after what happened in there. I wished none of that day had happened, and I was in my pink daybed wrapped up in my comforter that smelled like home.

Instead, I was in this unfamiliar place, with donated pajamas, red scratchy blankets, and another borrowed bed.

The room was small. A twin bed with metal frame. The sheets smelled like industrial detergent and nothing like home. I lay there in the dark, listening to unfamiliar sounds—doors closing, voices murmuring, footsteps in hallways I couldn't see.

I didn't know it at the moment, but that was where I would spend the next month of my life.

Looking back, I see something now that I couldn't see at fourteen. That was the room where I had to stand on my own. The first room I entered without Brian, without anyone.

And even though I was scared, I was okay.

It wasn't a room I wanted, but it's part of the house I carry.

The room that showed me I was brave.

The Room with
Wicker Furniture

I spent a month at the children's center, sleeping in another room that wasn't mine. In my memories, that place feels dark, as if the light was never strong enough to reach the corners. There was school during the week, church on Sundays, every meal in the dining room, and sleep under scratchy blankets... all in donated clothes.

The whole place carried a sense of doom and gloom, but there were actually a couple of bright spots: small, unexpected moments of joy in the middle of everything.

One of them was an event sponsored by the National Football League. A few of us were bused to a huge convention center where the NFL was hosting an interactive fan day. There were games, prizes, food everywhere, and even professional football players signing memorabilia. I wasn't a huge sports fan, but even I knew this was a big deal.

I was also chosen to go to a Cirque du Soleil performance, one of their early touring shows. I remember sitting there, completely blown away. It was the most incredible show I had ever seen. These were small moments of wonder in the middle of everything.

It had been a month since the day I turned my mother in to the police when the courts decided I could be released to a family member. My stepfather's mom, Alatha, stepped up to take me in. Her place was just a few blocks from my high school, which meant I didn't have to change schools. Thank God for small miracles. For the rest of that school year, about six months total, I lived with her. To say I'm grateful doesn't even begin to cover it.

Alatha had a spare bedroom that I stayed in, and in contrast to the room at the center, this one was almost too bright. There was a twin bed with a fluffy comforter, a dresser, a rocking chair, and a small nightstand with a lamp beside the bed. All of the furniture was white wicker. This wasn't exactly my style but, compared to where I had been the past month, it might as well have been the Lincoln Bedroom at the White House.

The whole time at Alatha's, I struggled with emotional outbursts. There was a day I wanted to skip class and hang out with some of my friends in the music room of my school. I wrote myself a note, forging Alatha's signature, that excused me from whatever class I wanted to skip. Probably English. I hated that teacher. When my friends and I inevitably got caught, I confidently presented the note to the administration. It was such an obvious forgery. I didn't stand a chance.

The school called Alatha to report that I would receive detention for truancy, and all the feelings I had bottled up my whole life—shame, rejection, judgment, insecurity, and the certainty that I had fucked up and wasn't lovable—all boiled up, and I began to cry hysterically.

Alatha had to pick me up from school early, and I spent the rest of the day curled up on the floor of my bedroom, sobbing. I didn't know what panic attacks were back then, but looking back, I'm almost certain that's what was happening. I cried for hours. I could not be consoled. I was screaming, "I want to go home!" over and over and over again for hours. A broken record of grief.

I was likely suffering from depression, though no one was talking about that in the 90s. Finding comfort felt impossible, even in that bright, safe space. Alatha tried so hard to make her condo feel like home for me, but years of instability had taught me never to settle in and never to let anyone get too close. The rug always gets pulled out, eventually.

Alatha never heard how much her kindness meant to me during that impossible time. Having a safe place to land while my mother and I went through the judicial process meant everything to me. I only hope now that, even though I was an emotional mess, she knew how deeply I loved her.

During those six months, my mother and I attended court-ordered therapy.

I have no memory of those sessions, good or bad. I just remember an office that looked exactly like I would have imagined it: dark furniture, a navy-blue couch with small flowers, dark carpet, and a coffee table with us on one side and the therapist on the other.

All of those details, and not a single memory of the conversations that took place in that room.

Did we talk about the beating? About Brian? About all the years before that night? I don't know. Maybe we did. Maybe I blocked it out on purpose. Maybe nothing real was ever said. I sat there week after week, and somehow, none of it stuck.

It was just over six months before the court decided that my mother was "reformed," and I was to return home.

Reformed.

How they came to that determination, I will never know. Was it from the therapist's notes? Do they use a prescribed timeline? So many bruises meant an equal number of weeks of therapy? God only knows.

I had a hard time believing any reform had happened, but I had no say at the age of fourteen. No one asked me if I felt safe. No one asked me if I wanted to go home. The system decided and I had to live with it.

I guess I don't even know what her reform was supposed to look like, but I know that I had to believe that she had changed. I had to believe that I could go home and that something, anything, might feel normal again. Even if it wasn't safe, safety had never been my baseline, anyway.

I packed my belongings in that room full of wicker furniture and returned home.

Suddenly, I was back in that room with the pink daybed, the mirrored closet doors, and the dresser we painted together only a year before. It was all the same as I had left it. Same furniture. Same walls. Same carpet.

But the air was different. Heavy. Watchful. I was different.

I set my bag down on the bed and looked around. This was supposed to be my room, my space. But it felt like stepping into a museum of someone else's life. The girl who lived here before didn't exist anymore.

I lived in that room for three more years, but it never felt safe, and it never felt like mine again.

I learned to sleep lightly. To listen for footsteps. To keep my door cracked so I could always hear what was coming. I became an expert at reading the temperature of that house before I even entered a room.

That distance between who I was before and who I became after is a gap I could never fully close.

The Room Where
Love Found Me

I'm happy to say that things changed at home. Our mother never hit us again. For better or worse, she upgraded to psychological abuse.

She made a point of trying to make me feel guilty for any behavior she couldn't correct, like hitting us had been the only option, and without corporal punishment, the house would dissolve into anarchy.

I still lived in fear of her anger and rejection, so I toed the line as best as I could. But Brian? He got in trouble constantly. He was arrested on numerous occasions: once for stealing a case of beer from the local gas station (and then hiding in the dumpster, which didn't work because they watched him climb in). He was caught trespassing on the roof of a Taco Bell, stole cars from friends' parents, and stole pipe fittings to make weed pipes before selling them at school. He dropped out of high school in his senior year and moved out a few days shy of his eighteenth birthday.

And who was responsible for these crimes? According to our mother, I was. Because she had "no way" to punish Brian, he got to run wild all over town. His behavior was always my fault.

Three days after I graduated from high school, I moved back in with Alatha. According to the United States government, I was an adult now, though some days I still don't feel like one. I had remembered her home as a haven for me when I was fourteen, and she offered me the same refuge again: a place to stay that wasn't home.

She had only one rule: I had to be home every night. No sleeping out. In hindsight, it was a perfectly reasonable rule for an eighteen-year-old living rent-free.

At the time? Rude.

I didn't think it would ever be an issue, though. I had no boyfriend, and no prospects, and figured my sleepover days were behind me.

But then, I met Kevin.

We met at Rock'n Java, a coffeehouse in Costa Mesa that was open 'til midnight. There were pool tables and outdoor seating and, as none of us were old enough for bars yet or had our own place to entertain, my friends and I hung out there a few nights each week. We drank too much coffee, played pool, and flirted shamelessly with cute boys.

One summer night, I showed up after my shift at a local restaurant and found my friends were already there, hanging out with another group. They had taken some of the outside tables and pushed them together to make one big group, creating an island in the middle of the patio. Kevin sat on the far end of this makeshift island and I noticed him immediately.

Ooh, girl, was he cute.

Something about him still reminds me of Matt Damon, even if I'm the only one who sees it. But even more than that, he was funny and had this troublemaker smirk that made you want to know every story he kept tucked behind it. *Swoon.*

We started talking, and he told me he worked at a restaurant making balloon animals.

Wait, what? That's a job?

Kevin sensed my disbelief and asked me for my favorite color. "Blue," I said. He told me to close my eyes, and I did. Seconds later, he handed me a blue balloon twisted into a flower with a green stem and leaf coming off the side. Damn. To an eighteen-year-old girl, that is *chef's kiss.*

We talked all night. Literally. We drove to the beach, sat in the sand, and talked until sunrise. I had never felt both so comfortable and so vulnerable with someone I had just met. Alatha was away for the weekend, and I could actually spend the night out with him without her knowing that I didn't come home.

From that day on, almost every day was spent together. Coffee shops, movies at his parents' house, parties with each other's friends. And, of course, some heavy make out sessions. Kevin had a small room upstairs in his house that had been converted into his hangout room. He had a giant lounge chair, television, and a tank where he kept his bearded dragons. We spent a lot of time up there "hanging out".

But I was still a good Christian girl and had maintained my virginity, although I was trying pretty hard to give that away. Kevin was respectful to the point of frustration, turning me down more than once, waiting until he felt I was absolutely sure I was ready.

And finally, one night, it was time. Cue the lights, cue the soundtrack... As Kevin still lived at home, and I was still living with Alatha, some hijinks were required to make this happen. We decided we would do the deed at his place after dinner with his parents. How romantic. As soon as dinner was over, we said our thank yous to his mom and headed to his bedroom to "watch a movie."

We stood awkwardly in Kevin's childhood bedroom and giggled quietly as we started to kiss, trying not to be heard by his parents down the hall. We climbed into his twin bed while Tommy Boy played on the TV. Then, gently, with a lot of checking in to make sure I was okay, Kevin made me a woman.

Finally.

I woke up curled against him, full of butterflies, until the morning light snapped us both into a panic. His parents were already up and moving around the house.

Shit!

We fell asleep in each other's arms, which would have been so sweet if it weren't such a terrible accident. I needed to leave without his parents knowing I was there. Kevin bounced into the kitchen to create a diversion. Casual and cool, he distracted his parents, while I slipped out through the garage, to my car, and drove myself home to Alatha's.

I drove home smiling ear to ear until I walked through the front door at Alatha's house.

Shit, again.

I had completely forgotten about Alatha and her one rule: No sleeping out.

Alatha was up and waiting, standing in the entryway. Her arms crossed over her chest, with her face curled up as tightly as it would go. I tried the excuses. "I fell asleep at Stacey's house. We were watching a movie. I just woke up this morning. I'm so sorry, it'll never happen again..." She let me go on and on, then sharply said, "No." She knew exactly where I'd been. She had been scared sick all night, worried about me when I didn't come home. And as it turns out, she knew where Kevin lived and had a family member drive by early that morning to see if my car was in front of his house.

Well, fuck. I was totally busted.

She told me to pack my things and get out. Just like that, I lost the only safe harbor I had known. And honestly, I couldn't even be mad. I had broken her one rule.

I was alone now. And homeless.

I was eighteen years old, sitting in my car, crying in a panic, running through my options. I couldn't go home, and I couldn't afford my own place. And then I remembered Matthew.

Matt was a friend from high school who always had an open-door policy. "If you ever need a place to crash," he told me more than once. I had never taken him up on it before, but now I was out of options.

Matt and his dad lived in an apartment complex a few miles from where I went to high school. They were not the cleanest people, with mail and magazines stacked on every surface, laundry spread all over the floors in the bedrooms, and Matt's dad wearing nothing but tight white underwear most of the time. It was still a better option than living in my car, or worse, back home.

I stood at their door with my bags, unsure what I was walking into. Would this last a week or a month? I wasn't sure if I'd ever have a real home again.

Matt opened the door, took one look at my face, and said, "Come in. You can stay as long as you want."

And for the first time in a long time, I believed it.

Matt and his dad, who insisted I call him Dad, became family to me. Matt and I spent almost every day and night together, as friends, playing Sim City, smoking from a huge bong while sitting on the couch on the deck, and sharing our most sacred secrets.

We had good times in that apartment. Late nights with friends, tons of wine coolers, stories, and laughter. It was messy and chaotic and I loved it.

Kevin and I continued dating for the next few months, until he left for college in the fall. Kevin had been accepted to a university in Colorado before we met. He told me on multiple occasions that had we met two months sooner, he would have gone to college in California instead. Was it true? Who knows. But the sentiment stayed with me: that I was worth staying for, even if the timing was all wrong.

As fall approached, we both felt it coming: the end. He was leaving for college, for everything that came next, and I was staying behind, in every way imaginable, trying to figure out what came next.

Once he left for Colorado, we both knew it wasn't sustainable. He was off on this grand adventure, and I didn't have a clue what I was doing next. We broke up shortly thereafter, and eventually lost contact. Not in anger or heartbreak, but in the way young people do when they know something beautiful has run its course. I didn't cry when we said goodbye. I just held on to what he'd given me: proof that I was worth wanting.

For most of my adult life, I wanted to believe that someone like Kevin would save me. That a man would see me for who I wanted to be. Not who my mother saw, and not even who I saw most days. I wanted someone to recognize that I was funny, kind, and generous. That I had an optimistic soul, always searching for humor and joy, even in the worst situations. That I could one day become a good wife and a loving mother.

I continued to pray for that. I hoped for that person who would see all of that and save me, because I didn't believe for one second that I could save myself.

What I found at Matt and Dad's apartment wasn't romantic love. It was something I'd never known, something even more rare: unconditional acceptance. I got to just be me. No performance, no fear, no having to earn my place.

Matt became one of the people I'm most grateful for. That strange apartment, with Dad in his underwear and secrets shared over a bong on the deck. It wasn't picture-perfect, but it was real love that didn't depend on me giving up part of myself in return.

In the room where I fell in love with Kevin, I learned what it felt like to be wanted.

In the room where Matt and Dad loved me just as I was, I started to believe I might actually be worth keeping.

It would take years to fully understand this, but the truth was already forming: I was the one I had been waiting for all along.

Part Two

The Room at The Bus Station

I lived with Matt and Dad in that messy apartment for a year. And for the first time in my life, I had something resembling peace. But safety can be a strange thing when you've never really known it. Instead of grounding me, it made me restless. The quiet was too loud. The calm felt temporary. And somewhere inside me, I was still waiting for the floor to give out.

I needed an escape. A fresh start. Somewhere far away from everything I'd ever known.

And that's when a memory surfaced: Eric.

Back in high school, my mother used to bring us to church at least twice a week. Brian and I went to the youth group while our mom stayed in the big chapel. That's where I met Eric. I've always been a sucker for kind eyes, and that almost-smirk people have. The kind of smirk that's not quite trouble, but definitely leaning in that direction. Eric had that smile.

We went to different high schools, and since his family was deeply involved in the church, it was a very innocent relationship: long phone calls, hand-holding, youth group pizza nights, the kind of thing that fizzles into friendship when one person is hooked on chaos and the other is hooked on Jesus.

I remember trying to make him fudge for Valentine's Day. Why? I couldn't even tell you. Maybe he mentioned he liked fudge? More likely, I was just desperate to give him a reason to keep me around. Well, I made it, but I must have missed a step in the recipe, because it was... gritty. It tasted like chocolate paste mixed with sand. But being someone who never quits—even when I should—I packed it into a small heart-shaped container and gave it to him.

Always a gentleman, he ate it. I can't imagine what he must have been thinking, chewing on the crunchy fudge while smiling politely. But he did it. And that small act of kindness—eating terrible fudge without complaint—probably mattered to me more than it should have. I was always looking for proof that someone would choose me, even when I made it hard.

Eric and his family moved to Iowa before our senior year, but we stayed in touch. We were internet pen pals in the early days of dial-up, trading emails about nothing and everything.

He knew all about my time with Alatha, Kevin and the breakup, my life with Matt and Dad. He'd tease me sometimes, joking that I should move to "the great state of Iowa," always laughing at his own joke. But I wasn't laughing. I was listening.

Because Iowa wasn't really about Eric. Not entirely. It was about having somewhere—anywhere—to point myself toward that wasn't here. Eric was just the one friendly face in a place where nobody knew my story. Where I could walk into a room without carrying every version of myself I'd ever been. He was the excuse I needed to get out, dressed up as a destination.

One night, I sat on the couch outside with a giant bong at my feet, staring into the darkness. I was nineteen, sleeping on someone's couch, working a job that was going nowhere. California felt like a room I had already searched a hundred times, finding nothing but the same pain in different corners.

I needed to get out. Out of that state. Out of that life. Out of my own skin. And then, with almost no thought at all, I decided I was moving to Des Moines, Iowa.

Because, why wouldn't I?

Des Moines was the only other place in the world where I knew someone. After a lifetime of feeling like everything around me could collapse at any second, Iowa sounded like the clean slate I desperately needed. In Iowa, I could be anyone I wanted to be. I didn't know a single thing about Des Moines—it might've taken me a full minute just to find it on a map—but once the idea hit me, that was it. And by now you probably know: when I make a decision, I act.

A few weeks later, I bought a ticket and sat on the old, urine-colored linoleum floor of the Greyhound bus station with my high school friends—laughing, then crying, then laughing again at the absurdity of it all. It was 1998; no one had a cell phone, the internet barely existed, and I was about to climb onto a bus and ride halfway across the country, alone.

I had two suitcases and nine dollars in my pocket.

The bus station was massive, with at least a hundred people inside. Some sat in long rows of connected metal chairs, their noses buried in books and newspapers. They waited quietly for buses to Salt Lake City, Sacramento, or wherever else the night might take them. Others drifted aimlessly, shuffling from one spot to another, going nowhere at all.

In my memory, the room is shadowed and the strangers in it are faceless, colorless, just background. But my friends and I, huddled on that dirty floor, are vibrant, as if we're under a spotlight.

It's a miracle that the universe gifted me those people during my high school years, and I'm so fortunate that we're all still friends to this day. They have always been a light to me. In every room they exist in, no matter how heavy the air feels, they glow.

I can still see their tear-stained faces as I boarded the Greyhound bus. I held it together until the bus hit the highway. Then I cried quietly in my seat and never looked back. I was leaving it all behind: my family, my childhood, my people. I was going to find my way forward, leaving everything that happened in California at the border.

I was leaving behind every beating, every move and every time I had to pack a bag in the middle of the night. I was leaving behind my mother's voice telling me I ruined everything. I was leaving behind the girl who believed she wasn't worth keeping.

Or at least, I hoped I was.

It took a couple of days before I finally reached my new life in the Midwest. The bus wound its way through Las Vegas, Denver, Omaha... cities I'd only ever seen in movies or on maps. Before that bus, I had never even left California—except for one summer in Oklahoma when I was five and occasional trips to the river in Arizona with a friend's family.

When the bus pulled into Las Vegas, I stepped off during the layover and stood under the lighted canopy on Fremont Street. The lights were everywhere—flashing, spinning, brighter than anything I'd ever seen. I stood tall and felt like a Hollywood star—never mind that I was broke, never mind that I was running.

For just a moment, under all those lights, I wasn't the girl from the messy apartment or the children's home. I was just someone passing through, on my way to somewhere else.

And that felt like everything.

The Room Where I
Got Married

I was so thankful for Eric when I got to Des Moines. He let me drive his car, helped me find a place to live and a job, and introduced me to his friends. We were never meant to be a couple: I was still chaotic, and he was still into Jesus.

He ended up marrying a local Christian radio deejay, and we all stayed friendly until I moved out of the state in 2005.

One friend Eric introduced me to was Tom. He was sweet and innocent, tall, and had the softest green eyes. He bears a slight resemblance to Ross from the show Friends. Tom and I started dating, and we fell hard and fast. After just a couple of months spending all our free time together, we were spooning on a futon in his mom's house when he pulled me close, took my hand, and quietly asked me to marry him. I said yes. At only nineteen, we were in love.

We were so stupid.

I had only been in Iowa for a few months when Tom and I took a road trip to California. Over two days, we took turns behind the wheel of our little teal Geo Prizm driving through the midwest, the rockies, the deserts and finally into Southern California.

I introduced Tom, by then my fiancé, to my family and friends over the course of a couple of days. People were surprised by the rushed engagement, but I've never been someone who lets something like that deter me.

On our way back east, we made a stop in Vegas. I wanted to show Tom the lights on Fremont Street, the place where I'd felt like a star just months before.

And then, standing under those lights, we looked at each other and made one of the biggest decisions of our lives, on a whim.

We decided to just go ahead and get married. There wasn't much thought or planning. We didn't even change into something resembling a gown or suit. I wore denim overalls and a long-sleeve t-shirt. Tom was wearing American Eagle jeans with a pullover sweatshirt.

Tom and I said our vows in a small chapel off the Strip, with witnesses we'd met five minutes earlier. No friends, no family, and no one even knew until days later. But we were still excited to "honeymoon" in Vegas, or at least spend one night celebrating this monumental event. And, well, to consummate the marriage. For Tom, it was his first time. For me, not so much.

What we didn't know was that to check into a hotel or casino in Las Vegas, someone in your party had to be over 21 years old. We were both only nineteen, so we could get married, but couldn't get a room anywhere on the Strip. We tried Circus Circus, thinking that would be our best shot, but no. Without a responsible adult, we were turned away. So, we found a motel. The kind that probably charges by the hour.

The room had brown carpet, a king-sized four-poster bed made of dark wood, matching nightstands, a dresser, and, of course, mirrors on the ceiling. It smelled musty, the sheets were beige, and it was certainly not the honeymoon suite either of us had envisioned. But we were young, in love, and husband and wife. So, we made the best of it.

By then, I'd only been to Vegas twice: the first feeling like a movie star, and the second for my wedding in denim overalls, looking more like a farmer than a bride.

Tom and I didn't have a terrible marriage, but it wasn't a good one either. We were just so young and came from two very different worlds. He was from a Christian family with divorced parents, and his father was battling cancer when we met. You know my story up to here, so you can imagine that I wasn't a natural homemaker and had no clue how to be someone's wife. While we didn't fight a whole lot, we also didn't connect.

I believe now that I had a hard time trusting that any relationship could work. If I was happy, I needed to break it before it naturally fell apart and broke my heart. That way, I was in control. So I pushed Tom away every chance I got—asking for more attention, more support, more affection, while giving nothing in return. I'd pick fights over nothing.

Question his love. Test him to see if he'd stay. And when he did stay, I'd wonder what was wrong with him that he'd put up with me.

Tom's father, who had always been so kind to me, passed away about a year into our marriage.

I watched Tom break in ways I didn't know how to fix. Neither of us knew how to process something so life-shattering. Tom was devastated, and I was not equipped to be the support he needed while he grieved. I didn't know how to sit with someone else's pain when I was still drowning in my own.

We never stood a chance.

Tom and his dad were lifelong Chicago Cubs fans. We had a set of shot glasses that traveled from apartment to apartment with us, intended for the father-son whiskey shots they would take when the Cubs finally won the World Series. Even though Tom and I hadn't spoken in more than ten years by the time the Cubs took the series in 2016, I still got choked up thinking about how bittersweet that moment must have been for him.

A few months after his father passed, Tom and I, and his siblings took a trip to Chicago to honor his memory. They wanted to take him to a Cubs game the way they'd always planned.

Now, what I'm about to tell you is purely hypothetical. A story that may or may not have happened, told in a way that protects the innocent.

Chicago was about a five hour drive from Des Moines. We rented a large van and all traveled together. We stayed in a hotel with floor-to-ceiling windows overlooking the Chicago River. We packed the urn carrying Tom's dad's ashes and he stayed in our room. We narrated the whole trip for him, detailing the adventures we had while he waited for us in the hotel.

The day of the game would be his big day out.

That morning, there was a tiny grape jelly jar on our room service tray. I dumped the jelly into the garbage and then washed and thoroughly dried the jar while Tom had a moment alone with his father's ashes. Once the jar was ready, Tom opened the urn and the bag inside, and used a clean spoon from breakfast to scoop just enough ashes to fill that little jar.

Tom's dad went everywhere with us that day: the Married with Children fountain, the Sears Tower, tucked next to a slice of deep-dish pizza. Then he made it into Wrigley Field in someone's cargo shorts pocket. We took pictures of the little jar "watching" the game with binoculars pressed against the glass—the kind of dark humor his father would have loved.

By the fifth inning, the sky started to rumble and it started to rain. We stayed in our seats as people shuffled out, looking for cover from the showers. The rain changed the energy and, one by one, we all stopped laughing. Tom and his sisters sat quietly, letting the rain come down, sharing a moment with their father's memory.

Then the game was called for rain.

Someone, I can't say who, took this opportunity to sprint down to the railing, open the little jelly jar, and pour out its contents.

The ashes, heavy with the rain, found a new home in the dirt.

It was chaotic, emotional, possibly illegal, and somehow perfect. Maybe that's why the memory feels so vivid; it was the closest we ever got to feeling like a real family.

Two years after our Vegas chapel wedding, Tom handed me a letter asking for a divorce. Honestly, it was probably the smartest thing we ever did. We ended it before there were children to break.

The split itself was simple, even if it broke my heart. We sat with a yellow legal pad and wrote down every possession in our little one-bedroom apartment:

Living room TV – Tom
Big couch – Tom
Smaller couch – April
Christmas decorations – April

On it went until everything was accounted for. I moved out of our apartment and Tom kept our Bichon Frise, Henry. It was amicable, as far as divorces go; no big blowups, no tabloid-worthy drama. Just two kids who had tried to build a life before either of us had learned how to build ourselves. And because we ended things so peacefully, we stayed friends as best we could.

When we finalized the divorce though, I still felt like a failure. But now I see it was the first crack in the old foundation I'd been standing on—the beginning of learning that sometimes you have to let something fall apart before you can build it right.

The Wedding

A few months after Tom and I said our vows in that little Vegas chapel, we found out we weren't officially married.

At our tax appointment, the accountant looked up and said, "You're missing a signature."

I felt my stomach drop. Tom and I looked at each other.

Just like that, our marriage was reduced to paperwork, or lack of it. We weren't married. We'd been living together, sleeping together, calling ourselves husband and wife for six months. And none of it counted.

In the community we were in, we could not let this get out. We were essentially "living in sin."

Looking back, this could have been our way out. A clean break, no divorce needed. We could have laughed it off and gone our separate ways.

But we were in too deep. Or maybe we just didn't know how to walk away from something we'd already committed to, even if the commitment had not been legal.

We decided nobody needed to know. We just had to actually get married before word got out.

We started planning in secret. We knew that if we just popped into our local courthouse, our news would be printed in the Des Moines Register, followed by a lot of questions. We had to get creative. After some research, we found a little chapel across state lines that could marry us for under $300. We immediately booked a little getaway and drove the five hours to a slightly nicer hotel, with no mirrors on the ceiling, for our planned—but still secret—second wedding.

The judge who processed our marriage license could barely keep a straight face, but he approved it. The next morning, I dressed in an ivory cardigan sweater set with a soft pink, knee-length skirt. Tom wore a pair of navy Dockers and a beige polo.

Standing in that chapel with another set of strangers as our witnesses, I felt this strange mix of embarrassment and relief. This should have felt romantic. Instead, it felt like damage control.

But the moment Tom took my hand, I told myself it meant something. That this time, it would count.

We were finally, officially, married.

I don't remember the exact date of either wedding anymore, but I'll never forget the place. Because if you're going to have a secret second wedding before you're twenty, there's only one place to do it: the Chapel of Love, Mall of America, Minneapolis, Minnesota.

The Room with
the Electric Fence

Before I learned how to rebuild, I spent eight years in the Midwest trying to burn it all down.

This room, in particular, is a wild one. One I can't close off or paint over. It smells like gasoline, rain, and manure. It's loud, stupid, and beautiful. It's the room that taught me that sometimes surviving joy is its own kind of feral bravery. The music is too loud, laughter echoes off the walls, and danger is tucked into every corner. The air itself buzzes with energy, alive and electric, and too bright to last.

This was Iowa before everything fell apart.

During the early years in Iowa, I spent nearly all my free time with Tom and our friends Nick, Troy, and Jon. We all lived in the same apartment building, across the hall from each other, like the show Friends, but with more bloodshed and fewer witty comebacks. Tom and I were in one apartment and Nick in another, with Troy and Jon just down the hall.

Most nights we'd order pizza and pile into someone's living room to play N64: GoldenEye or Tetris, controllers in hand, talking shit and laughing late into the night.

One night, I was sitting in an office chair, eyes locked on the screen, when Nick walked past and gave the chair a hard spin. He was just messing around, but the chair whipped halfway, flipping backwards. Everything went in slow motion as I fell, my elbow landing perfectly in Tom's drink. Glass shattered, and there was blood everywhere.

"Oh shit," Nick said.

"Oh, shit!" I said, louder.

We didn't have health insurance, and we obviously didn't have anything resembling adult supervision. So once the bleeding finally stopped, and it took a while, we slapped some Steri-Strips on it and called it a day. To this day, I have a four-inch scar on the back of my arm that I lovingly call my "Nick Scar." Ironically, Nick Scar is his actual name—first and last. You can't make this shit up.

We went storm chasing when tornadoes rolled through. We rode ATVs on Nick's family's farm until someone got hurt—usually me. We held onto Troy's bumper and "skied" behind his car on icy roads, our boots sliding across packed snow at thirty miles an hour.

We were nuts, and we knew it.

One night, we were out chasing a storm in Troy's Oldsmobile. The sky was dark but almost green. The air was humid and creepy, and so still it felt like the world was holding its breath. We were driving through a small town that had just been hit by a small tornado; trees were down in the road, sirens were blaring, and we were running low on gas.

While stopped at a gas station, Troy put the nozzle into the tank, but nothing happened. Concerned, he went inside and came back out moments later, with his hands up as if to say, "No gas here." The pumps had stopped working during the storm.

As we pulled away to find the next station, we heard a huge BOOM! We all jumped in our seats, then immediately laughed once we realized Troy had driven off with the nozzle for the fuel pump still in the tank. The hose from the pump was now whipping in the wind behind us like a kite tail.

That's how it always was with us: chaos followed by hysterical laughter. Fear melting into the best parts of friendship.

Nick's family farmed cattle and corn in the town of Earlham, about half an hour west of Des Moines. I loved that place. The mud, the ATVs, and the kind of dirt that looked like mud but definitely didn't smell like it.

One day, we were riding ATVs past a creek that ran through the property. Nick saw a green barrel resting on the bank of the creek and dared me to try and ride it, staying upright as long as I could. I never say no to a dare. So we climbed off our ATVs, ducked through the electric fence that kept the cattle in the pasture, and headed down to the creek.

I thought I was hot shit climbing onto that green barrel. It was about the size of an outdoor garbage can, easy enough for me to swing a leg over and sit down on it. I straddled it carefully, balancing myself on some rocks with one foot. I pushed my foot into the rocks slightly to free myself from the muddy bank, then picked my foot up to ride the barrel and complete the dare. Only, as soon as I lifted my foot, the barrel rolled onto its side, throwing me into the creek.

I landed on a pile of rocks and laughed so hard I cried. I'll admit, there may have been a few tears of pain mixed in. I climbed out of the creek while blood trickled down my leg. The boys made sure I was okay and then laughed until they were practically rolling on the ground.

At that point, I decided I'd had enough of the creek, the farm, and these stupid boys for now, and headed back toward the house to have a drink with Nick's mom instead.

As I trudged toward the ATVs, soggy and bleeding, I just needed to climb back through that electric fence to take the quick ride to a Band-Aid, a cocktail, and a shower. When I ducked between two electrified wires of the fence, I accidentally bumped the middle of my back on the wire above me.

I was soaking wet.

The electricity from that quick tap of the wire jolted through my entire body. The literal shock of it surprised me so much that it threw me forward... right into the string of electric fence below me.

Another jolt shot through me, launching me back up into the wire above. Down. Up. Down. Up. I was trapped in an electric ping-pong game until I finally fell over and was released.

Now I was wet, bleeding, and electrocuted. That was more than enough for me that day.

I went back to the house, freshly humbled, where Nick's mom took one look at me and handed me a towel, a drink, and a reason to laugh.

Man, I loved that farm.

Looking back, I can see what those days were really about. We weren't just being reckless. We were building something. A makeshift family held together by bad decisions and good timing. These boys weren't trying to fix me or save me. They just allowed me to show up, exactly as I was, and laughed with me through it all.

That was Iowa for me: reckless and real, stupid and sacred, all at once.

The Room That
Smelled Like Sulfur

The five of us: myself, Tom, Jon, Nick, and Troy, all worked together at the West End Diner, a retro spot on the edge of the west end of Des Moines where farmland stretched out in every direction. A few times a month, after closing the restaurant, we'd pile into Troy's car and find ourselves an adventure.

Fireworks were illegal in Iowa, but that didn't stop my friends and me from driving to Missouri every couple of months and stuffing the trunk of Troy's Oldsmobile with an absurd amount of explosives. You shouldn't be on a first-name basis with the guy at the firework shop in the next state. But we were.

One of our favorite "adventures" was to take Troy's Oldsmobile out to a dirt road and shoot off our Missouri haul: bottle rockets, roman candles, and mortars that shook the ground when they exploded. We were a traveling Fourth of July spectacular, and we never once considered that the farmers trying to sleep might not appreciate the show.

Every week or so, we'd pick a night, drive out to the country, and light up the sky. We had a CB radio in the car and one cell phone that was useless out there. There were no cell phone towers, no signal, and no help if we needed it.

One night, we were standing in the middle of a dirt road, surrounded by dark cornfields in the thick of summer, shooting off fireworks about a mile from a farmhouse. The air smelled like sulfur and burned cardboard.

Nick was laughing at something Troy said. Jon was setting up another mortar. I was holding a roman candle, watching the sparks arc into the black sky.

Then a set of headlights broke through the darkness. They were heading toward us. Fast. Another set appeared from the opposite direction, closing us in.

"Uh... guys?" Nick said.

We all saw it at the same time. They were not slowing down. It was obvious they were coming for us.

All five of us sprinted to the car and scrambled in: Troy in the driver's seat, me as front passenger, Nick, Tom, and Jon in the back. Troy pulled the lever on the dashboard, throwing it into drive, and slammed on the gas. I dropped to the floorboards, elbows on the seat, hands clasped in front of me like I was eight years old again.

God, please keep us safe. God, please keep us safe.

One set of headlights belonged to a white van that swerved directly in front of us and skidded to stop, sending up a cloud of dust and blocking our path. Troy hit the brakes so hard that the back of my head slammed against the dashboard. He pushed the lever up to shift into reverse, cranking his neck around, and the second car had already caught up, blocking us from behind.

We were trapped.

"Shit," Troy said in a panic. "Shit, shit, shit."

In the back seat, Nick, Tom, and Jon had gone completely silent.

Troy rolled down his window, his voice coming out in a rush. "We're sorry, man, we're so sorry, we were just—"

A large man had emerged from the van, his face twisted with rage as he lumbered toward the car. He didn't say a word. He just pulled his fist back and swung it through the open window, connecting hard with Troy's jaw.

Troy's head snapped to the side.

That's when we knew for sure. These men were not interested in apologies or explanations.

Troy yanked the shifter back into drive, cranked the steering wheel to the right as far as it would go, and started inching forward. He angled the car toward the narrow gap between the van and the ditch. I felt the sickening lurch as the wheels dropped off the road, then a violent bounce as they clawed their way back up on the other side of the van. Troy hit the gas, found the open road, and headed back toward town. We were flying.

Nobody spoke. The only sound was the engine screaming and Troy's ragged breathing.

The white van and the other car did not follow us. Thank God.

As we got closer to town, the cell phone finally connected to a tower. My hands were shaking so badly I could barely dial. I called 9-1-1, and when the dispatcher answered, I was out of breath, choking back tears.

"We need help. We were just attacked! We're heading toward the West End Diner. Please have someone meet us there!"

The police arrived shortly after we did. We told them everything: the headlights coming from both directions, the white van, the angry man, the punch. Okay, we told them *almost* everything.

Then the officer asked the question we were hoping to avoid: "What were you all doing out there on that dirt road in the middle of the night?"

Our shoulders slumped in unison. Troy slowly walked to the back of the car and popped open the trunk. It was filled to the top with illegal fireworks.

The officer's eyebrows went up, and his mouth twitched at the corners. *Was he smiling?* Yeah, he was definitely smiling. He confiscated every last one, stacking them carefully into his cruiser while we stood there in silence, our adrenaline finally starting to fade.

I don't think for one second that all of those fireworks made it back to the precinct. But who am I to judge?

That night should have been the end of our stupidity. But it wasn't. We just stayed far away from any farms.

A few years later, after I'd left the West End Diner, I worked as a bartender at Mickey's Irish Pub. The staff, and customers even, found new, stupid traditions to keep our lives exciting. As a group, we'd go play paintball and show up to work the next day covered in bruises. We had barbecues mid-week, after-hours parties when the bars closed, and an incestuous dating situation that everyone pretended not to notice.

Every summer, the staff from Mickey's gathered at the townhome of our friends, Adam and Stinky, for the annual slip-and-slide party.

They had a massive hill behind their place, and they'd buy a huge roll of industrial plastic from Home Depot and unroll it down the hill. They'd tap a keg, turn on the hose and pour dish soap across the plastic. With a running start we'd launch ourselves down that hill again and again like we had nothing to lose.

There was music blasting, usually thirty or forty people, tons of food, and a keg of beer. It was absolute chaos and a terrible idea, but it was so much fun.

Nobody ever thought to rake the lawn before laying down the plastic, so at least one person would end up sliced open by a sharp rock, a piece of glass, or some tiny chunk of metal hiding in the grass as they raced toward the bottom of the hill.

We never let injuries ruin the day. We'd rinse the wounds with hose water and dish soap, slap some duct tape over them, and launch ourselves back down the hill. It was redneck fun at its finest. If I could go back and relive one of those days, I totally would.

When I think about those ridiculous times in Iowa, what I remember isn't the fear or the blood or the scars. I remember the feeling that those people were my family. Even in the craziest, scariest moments, they always protected me, and they always made me laugh.

My Iowa family taught me the meaning of choosing your people. And as much as my time with them should have taught me how to be careful, it actually taught me how to live. We were fearless, maybe a little too fearless.

But I had adventures, and I had people who made me laugh all the way to my bones.

Their room is filled with warmth and, ironically, safety.

The Room Where My Mother Found Me

By early 2001, life in Iowa had settled into something resembling normal. I was waitressing, living in a duplex with my bartender friend Chad, and dating Jonathan. The wild adventures hadn't stopped completely, but they had become less frequent. We'd traded some of the chaos for routine: work shifts, after-work drinks, lazy Sundays.

The chosen family I'd built was still there, still solid, just quieter. Which is why when I woke up one morning in January feeling a little nauseous, I didn't think twice about calling them.

I didn't have the strongest work ethic and didn't love my job as a waitress, so I was always looking for a reason to call in sick for the lunch shift. This was a perfect opportunity. So I called my boss, told her I had a stomach virus, and then rooted myself back into my pillow and blankets, content that I didn't have to get out of my pajamas that day.

Chad was out of town that week, so I was home alone. I hate being sick alone. I wanted comfort, someone to care. I called Tom and asked if I could spend the day at his apartment just to have some company.

Funny twist: There were three roommates in that apartment: Tom, Jon, and Jonathan. I was dating Jonathan. Yes, my boyfriend and my ex-husband were roommates. Des Moines was a pretty small town.

I couldn't tell you why I called Tom instead of Jonathan. Maybe I saw Tom as more of an adult? Jonathan was a couple of years younger than us. Maybe I just needed the validation that Tom still cared about me? Maybe I did call Jonathan and just couldn't reach him? Honestly? I don't remember.

What I do know is I'm grateful that Tom said yes and even offered me his room. He was at work for the day, but his roommate, our friend Jon, would be home in case I needed anything.

What a peach, seriously. I could've been carrying some highly contagious, deadly bacteria (*spoiler: I was*), and he just opened up his home to me.

Happy to have somewhere to go that wasn't work, I pulled on Jonathan's oversized yellow fleece that I'd stolen from him, a pair of plaid flannel pajama pants, and my white Adidas with red stripes.

Their apartment was about a fifteen-minute drive from me, one that included one stop at the convenience store where I bought two small red Gatorades. I was so thirsty that I drank both in less time than it took me to get to their apartment.

It wasn't long before things started to go downhill. By the time I got to their block, I felt awful—so awful I had to pull over and throw up. Twice.

Thank God for Jon. He let me in and set me up for what was clearly going to be a day of misery. He brought me a hamper to vomit in (*picture that, a hamper!*) and piled on blanket after blanket as my fever rose and the chills set in. He brought me water when I cried for it and monitored me closely, updating Tom and Jonathan whenever they called to check in.

I had never been so sick in my entire life. Every inch of my body hurt. Not a dull ache of a fever, but something deeper. My bones were throbbing. My joints were tight and pounding. Even my skin hurt. My neck was the worst—stiff, tight, and searing. Every time I tried to lift my head, the pain shot straight up the back of my skull and exploded behind my eyes.

I kept trying to sip water, desperate for something to soothe the dryness in my mouth, but with every tiny swallow, my stomach would react. I'd never experienced thirst and nausea at the same time like I did that day.

By evening, it was a pretty shitty resemblance to Three Men and a Baby. Tom, Jon, and Jonathan were all taking care of me. I couldn't keep even a sip of water down, and at around six o'clock in the evening, roughly seven hours after I woke up feeling nauseous, I started seeing double.

I could see it in their faces—what I didn't want to admit: this wasn't just the flu. I heard Jonathan on the phone with his mother in the next room, his voice low and rushed. He told her all of my symptoms. I had been diagnosed with a chronic kidney condition two years earlier, and now they were afraid my kidneys were failing.

One by one, the guys came into the room and begged me to let them take me to a hospital. I refused. The thought of getting out of bed, going out into the cold, riding in a car, then facing the bright lights and chaos of a hospital, all felt like too much. But when they threatened to call an ambulance, I caved. All of the above sounded exhausting, but ambulance sounded even worse.

They bundled me up, helped me to the car, and drove me to the county hospital. I laid across Jonathan's lap in the backseat, shivering under a pile of coats and blankets. Every turn, every bump in the road sent waves of pain through my body. Tears slid down my face and dripped onto Jonathan's sweatpants. I couldn't wipe them away and I couldn't stop them. I was so scared.

This was not the flu. Something inside me knew that. I was too sick, in too much pain, too on fire, and freezing all at the same time. I didn't know where the bottom of this sickness was, but I had a feeling I wasn't there yet, and I was too exhausted to keep fighting.

The emergency room was a sensory nightmare. The lights were aggressively bright, noises blurred in and out. And then there were the chills. Violent, bone-rattling chills that shook my whole body. My teeth clattered so hard I thought they might chip.

I was admitted to the hospital with what the emergency room doctor assumed was dehydration from a nasty virus. Once they moved me into a room, my friends went home for the night. The nurse hung IV fluids, gave me Tylenol for the fever, and I finally drifted off to sleep around midnight.

What happened next lives in my memory like a fever dream. I probably don't *need* to share this part of the story, but it paints a picture of how bad things got overnight.

I wasn't asleep for long before I jolted awake with the immediate sense that I needed to use the bathroom. Like, *now*. I swung my weak legs off the bed and started hobbling toward the bathroom, using the wall to steady myself. Halfway there, I felt myself being jerked backward… *shit*. I was stuck, tethered to the IV pole that was plugged into the wall.

I couldn't drag it with me, and I couldn't figure out how to disconnect it from the wall.

My guts did not care about logistics. Knowing that I didn't have a lot of time before all hell broke loose, I panicked, grabbed the garbage can beside me, yanked down my pajama pants, and relieved myself right there in the middle of the room.

In that moment, sick and scared and sitting on a garbage can, I knew. This wasn't just a bad virus. Something was really, really wrong.

My memory cuts in and out here. But I must have made it back to bed as the nurses' notes confirmed that I was found there. Which means I probably just pulled my pants back on, climbed into bed, and went to sleep.

Covered in shit.

I should mention that I did not have a private room. I had a room-mate.

Can you even imagine this from her perspective? She wakes up in the middle of the night to a woman hunched over a garbage can like a hobbit, unloading her bowels, and then silently crawling back into bed.

I would like to take this moment to formally apologize to that poor woman. This was my last memory before waking up five days later.

A few hours after I relieved myself in the garbage can, a med student was completing pre-rounds and found me unresponsive. He called a code for an emergency response and I was rushed to the ICU. They started broad-spectrum antibiotics, hung more fluids, and performed a spinal tap, drawing fluid from my spine to see what was trying to kill me.

The diagnosis: bacterial meningitis.

Meningitis does not negotiate. It's ruthless, fast, and indiscriminate. Its incubation period is less than 24 hours. You can wake up feeling a little unwell one day and be dead the next. That's the kind of monster it is.

Tom was my emergency contact. He received a call telling him that I had taken a turn for the worse and the hospital needed to reach my family.

My mother didn't know I was sick, or that I had been taken to a hospital the night before. To her surprise, she received a call from a doctor 1,300 miles away telling her that her daughter was in a coma and slipping away. She was told that she should fly to Des Moines immediately, and they would do everything they could to keep me alive until she arrived.

The doctors were preparing her to say goodbye, as they had little hope. As imperfect a mother that she was, this is a nightmare phone call.

My mom called her own mother, my grandmother, and shared this shocking news. They both booked flights immediately—my mom from Southern California and my grandma from Salt Lake City—and were at my bedside before the end of the day. My heart still breaks thinking about them; each sitting alone on a plane, not knowing if they'd arrive in time to say goodbye.

When my mom was first brought into my room in the ICU, she didn't recognize me. My face was swollen, body covered in a bloody rash, with tubes and machines crowding the space around me. The bloating in my face was only a hint of what was happening inside: my brain was swelling, pressing against my skull with nowhere to go.

My mother reached into her wallet and pulled out a picture of me, a Glamour Shot from when I was fourteen. Remember Glamour Shots? They were basically the Snapchat or Instagram filters of their time. I had the big hair, bedazzled jean jacket, and way too much makeup. But to my mom, that photo was me. She taped it to the machine above my head so every doctor and nurse who walked in would see it.

I wasn't just a broken, swollen body in a bed, but a girl who laughed too loudly, filled rooms with her energy, and had a whole life away from those machines.

For the next five days, my mother, my grandmother, a circle of friends, and even some of their families, never left the hospital.

They sat, and they prayed. People from churches in three states prayed. Doctors and nurses prayed. And somehow, I survived.

The manager from the restaurant where I had called in sick sent trays and trays of food to the hospital every day, making sure no one in the waiting room went hungry. Members of the church I attended opened their homes, offering showers, spare bedrooms for naps, and quiet places to regroup before coming back to the hospital. Nobody sat alone.

This beautiful community I'd collected, friends, coworkers, church members, and their families, all came together. Many of them were meeting for the very first time, yet they were all connected by the same thread: a girl fighting for her life down the hall.

That bed in the ICU lives in my house of rooms too. It's not one I like to visit often, but when I do, it's not the machines or the fear that linger. It's the memory of my mother fighting for me to be seen, to be remembered, to still be her daughter, not just another patient in the ICU.

For all the ways she had failed me before, in that room, she fought for me. She made them see me.

It didn't erase the past, but it mattered.

In that room, for those five days, she was the mother I'd always needed.

Warning Signs of Meningitis

Meningitis is a medical emergency. If you or someone you know experiences these symptoms, seek immediate medical attention:

- Sudden high fever

- Severe headache that won't go away

- Stiff neck

- Nausea and vomiting

- Confusion or difficulty concentrating Sensitivity to light

- Rash that doesn't fade under pressure Seizures

Early symptoms can resemble the flu, but meningitis progresses rapidly. Trust your instincts. If something feels seriously wrong, get to a hospital immediately. It could save your life.

The Room Where
I Saw What
Remained

As I started to wake up in the hospital bed, I tried to rip out the tubes that were keeping me alive, so they strapped my wrists and ankles to the bed. I was restrained and wearing a diaper, because here's something no one tells you: people in comas still have bowel movements. How glamorous.

I was twenty-two years old.

When I finally woke up and began breathing on my own, I started talking almost immediately. Which makes total sense, if you know me at all, yet I had no short-term memory and couldn't hold a conversation. I repeated the same things over and over, complimenting people's shirts and teeth, but never saying anything deeper.

I would yell for popsicles for hours. The nurse would bring me one, I'd eat it, and then immediately start yelling for another. I also couldn't retain new information. The popsicles I was given were the kind with jokes on the sticks. I would read the question on one end, then the answer on the other. By the time I read the punchline, though, I'd already forgotten the setup. I'd read them again and again, never getting the joke.

That room is one that I can still smell. The sharpness of the bleach in the linens. The tang of the oral swab they used to clean my mouth and wet my palate while I was still on the ventilator.

The bloody rash covering my body had a name: DIC, Disseminated Intravascular Coagulation. Basically, my blood was clotting under my skin. The clotting had cut off circulation in the fingers on my left hand, the tip of my ring finger on my right hand, and in both of my legs from the knee down.

I can still see the care and compassion in the doctor's face when he told me they needed to amputate my fingers. He stood next to my bed, hands gently clasped in front of him, explaining what had happened and what needed to be done. His voice was calm. Kind. I didn't fully understand any of it. I just lifted my hand—fingers blackened and shriveled like overripe prunes—and simply said, "Okay."

The swelling in my brain had left me in a childlike state. The doctors told my friends and family that I would probably survive, but I wouldn't be the same. I struggled to process information, couldn't follow conversations, and all the parts of me that were quick, fiery, and full of wit felt distant and muted—like someone had turned down the volume on my soul.

Thankfully, I didn't fully grasp my deficits at the time. In a strange way, that may have saved me from devastation.

The doctor ordered pumps to place on my legs that restored blood flow and was able to save both of my legs and all ten of my toes. Thank God, because I love to wear sandals. But in the end, three fingers on my left hand were amputated, along with the tip of one on my right.

I spent a month in the hospital before I was stable enough to be flown by private medical jet from Iowa back to California, closer to my family for recovery. When I finally left the hospital, I was thirty pounds lighter, missing a few fingers, unable to walk, and barely able to use my hands. My left hand was wrapped in a bandage the size of a boxing glove while it healed from the amputation.

My mom, stepdad, and Chris—now eight years old—lived in a new house. They had moved to Fountain Valley shortly after I moved to Des Moines.

On my first night at my family's new house, my mom made my favorite dinner. Filet mignon, a baked potato with gobs of butter, sour cream, and grated cheddar cheese, with a side of broccoli topped with melted Velveeta cheese. Their dining room table was shaped like a booth in a restaurant, a bench that wrapped around two sides with chairs at the others. I was sitting in a wheelchair at the head of the table, a spot typically left open so people could walk past into the kitchen.

I quietly looked at my plate.

My mom, nervous and eager to please for once, watched me closely. When I didn't immediately dig in, she looked worried. I glanced at the plate, then up at her, and said, "Are you serious? You made me a steak?

How am I supposed to eat this?" Then I shook my bandaged mitt at her, reminding her that in no world could I cut up a steak right now.

We both burst out laughing so hard that we cried. Chris and my stepdad looked on with confusion, which made us laugh even harder. It was the comedic relief we needed.

I was still me. Even with six fingers, even in a wheelchair, I could still make us laugh when we needed it.

The first time I took a shower, my mom needed to help me. I had lost so much weight that my skin hung on my bones. It's awkward to undress in front of your mother at twenty-two years old, but I couldn't get in and out of the shower myself, so I had to push past the humiliation. She taped a Wonder Bread bag over the mitt still on my hand to protect it from the water, and she placed a white plastic lawn chair for me to sit in her walk-in shower.

Having only one hand available, she helped me undress, and we both could see my body in all its glory: my ribs protruding, a fresh scar where a chest tube had been inserted when my lung collapsed, marks from tape and bandages, bruises in all stages of healing across every limb. It was hard to look at.

I was hard to look at.

I absolutely hated to be that vulnerable with her. I had to let the same woman who had hurt me in so many ways see me like this, stripped down to skin and bone and need. Part of me hated giving her the satisfaction of being the hero in that moment, but I needed help, and she was the one there to provide it.

I learned that sometimes, no matter how complicated the history, there are moments when a girl still needs her mother to step in. This was one of those moments.

Years earlier, we would sit together as a family on Thursday nights and watch The Simpsons. It was a light-hearted weekly ritual I really loved. Standing there in front of the mirror, something suddenly looked hilariously familiar. In my raspiest voice, I croaked, "Listen here, Smithers!" and shook my Wonder Bread–covered fist at her.

We laughed again. Because even in that moment, with my body frail and my pride gone, I was still me.

Over the next few weeks, I slowly regained strength with the help of physical and occupational therapy. Every day was hard. I was physically exhausted and frustrated by every new thing I couldn't do. I needed help to get on and off the toilet, to move from one room to the next, to pull on my clothes. My muscles were constantly sore, either from therapy or from pushing myself to get stronger faster than my body would allow.

Then came the day the bandages were removed from my hand.

I lay on a table in the surgeon's office, staring at the wall instead of my arm. If I could have left the hand covered forever, I would have. Not seeing the hand meant the surgery never happened. I could still feel the fingers; it even felt as though I could still move them. The pain extended to what felt like the tip of a finger, where they told me I had none.

None of it made sense in my head, with my hand in the glove. But the false feeling that the fingers were still there was better than seeing the truth. They weren't. The surgeon unwrapped each layer of gauze one at a time until finally there was nothing left to peel away. I could feel the cold room air on my skin but couldn't bring myself to look toward my hand. The surgeon touched my arm and said softly, "I'll give you some time." He quietly stepped out of the room.

It was just me, my mom, and my new normal.

Still on my back, I lifted what was left of my hand and brought it into view in front of my face.

The pinky and thumb were still there, with only a small scab on the tip of my pinky, a clot still trying to heal. What was missing was the entire index finger, most of the middle finger, and half of the ring finger. Each leftover piece had been stitched closed with black threads.

I stared at it. My hand. Not my hand. Both true at once.

The disorientation hit first. Then the grief. Then the loss. My heart shattered in a way I didn't know was possible.

It was real. This was forever. I would never be the same as I was before I entered that room.

I looked over at my mom for support and she was there. She held me while I cried, saving her own tears for later. Well, a moment later anyway.

Because in the middle of my heartbreak, she said—almost reflexively, like she couldn't help herself—'When you have a baby, the first thing you look at is their ten fingers and toes.' Her voice cracked as soon as she said it.

I stopped crying. Just for a second. Just long enough to feel the old, familiar sting.

Yes, it was her grief, too, but I needed her to hold mine, not voice her own. Not then. Not yet.

In that instant, all the old hurt, disappointment, and disconnect came rushing back. We were us again. That brief, fragile spell where she had been my safety was broken. Maybe that wasn't fair to her, but I needed what I needed.

I couldn't stay in California. I couldn't stay in that house, in that dynamic, as that version of myself that needed her help to shower. I needed to get back to Iowa, back to my friends, back to the life where I could pretend I was fine.

As soon as I regained enough strength to care for myself, I got on a plane heading back east. I moved into the apartment with Jon, Jonathan, and—I shit you not—their new roommate, John. Tom had moved out, and a friend named John had taken his place.

The next few years were pretty rough. I bounced from job to job, apartment to apartment, boyfriend to boyfriend—still reeling from everything: my childhood, my divorce, and now this brush with death that had left me with a different body and a fractured sense of who I was supposed to be. I had no foundation of security or structure to fall back on. So I kept moving. Kept drinking. Kept pretending that forward motion was the same as progress.

I thought I was healing. But in reality, I was just learning how to remain broken.

The Lamp

When Tom and I divorced, I rented an apartment all by myself. I was twenty-one years old, and this was my first time living alone. I finally got to pick out everything. My bedding was floral, not the masculine dark green Tom had chosen. The prints on my walls were soft pastels. Everything in my bathroom smelled like me. *Like a girl.*

And then there was this lamp.

I bought it at the brand-new Hobby Lobby in Des Moines, back when the store felt more like a warehouse, chaotic, and overflowing with knick-knacks. I loved this lamp. It was tall and slender, a bit ornate, with a dark, brassy base and a tiny metal pull chain. The shade was a patchwork of jewel tones, with beads sewn along the edges. It looked way fancier than its under-twenty-dollar price tag.

I'll admit it was a weird thing to be attached to, but I adored that lamp. It followed me through every version of myself over the next five years: new bedding, new boyfriends, and new scents. It was always there, quietly doing its job, making everything around it glow.

And then one day, it just stopped working.

There was this tiny heartbreak, like a sigh. The reign of that beautiful, ornate lamp was over.

I carried it out to the dumpster behind my building and stood there for a moment, holding it. This lamp had seen me through so much. It had watched me learn how to be alone, how to choose things for myself, how to build a life that was mine.

I looked it over one last time and tossed it in. So long, beautiful lamp.

Years later, way too many years later, it hit me. Out of nowhere, in one of those random quiet moments when your brain decides to surface an old memory.

I never checked the bulb.

The Room I Won't
Fully Enter

The door to this next room still creaks like it's haunted, and the air inside is heavy. But you deserve to see the truth of it. Because some rooms don't smell like bleach or candlelight. Some rooms smell like fear.

This is one of them.

The years after the divorce and the meningitis were messy. I kept moving, kept drinking, kept finding any warm body or loud bar to quiet the noise inside me. I made choices for the moment and never the future. And because of those choices I had a certain reputation: I wasn't the girl you brought home, but the girl you called at two o'clock in the morning.

I truly believed that was all I was worth. And when you treat yourself that way, other people follow your lead.

There is a certain room from that time I will not fully walk into. A room that should not exist. I cannot say I have healed from it. But what happened there changed me in ways I am still learning to name.

The images come back in flashes of memories, glimpses, moments. Confusion. Fragments I try to outrun: waking up in an unfamiliar room, bright lights, a hospital, questions I could not answer, a detective's calls I could not return. The feeling of dread and shame. Days when I could not eat, could not sleep, could not shower enough times to feel like myself again.

I will not retell every detail. Some stories are mine alone to hold. But I will tell you this: the girl who eventually walked out of that room learned to carry a weight she should never have had to.

I carried a deep shame that was never mine, though I wore it like it was.

After that room, my drinking got even worse. My recklessness grew. I convinced myself that I had somehow asked for what had happened.

I don't believe that anymore. But it took a long time to come back to myself.

When I tried to tell the story at first, not everyone believed me. I was cornered in the bar where I worked, berated, and told I was ruining someone's life. I was told no one would believe me because of who I was and the mistakes I had made.

They made me the villain in my own assault.

So, I stopped telling the story. I dropped the charges. Not because I wanted to. Not because it wasn't true. But because survival, then, meant silence.

But I survived.

I have come to a place of peace and forgiveness, even for myself. I protected myself the only way I knew how.

On the rare occasion that the room visits me, I still feel small. But I remind myself: I am the girl who walked out of that room. And I am safe now.

I will not carry shame anymore. I will only carry her strength.

I honor the girl who entered that room and the pieces of her that did not come out. The parts of her that believed the world was fundamentally safe, that her body was entirely her own, that trust was something freely given. She left those pieces behind so she could carry herself forward.

She deserved better than that room. But she survived it.

And that matters.

Part Three

The Room Where I Was Chosen

I worked a lot of odd jobs in Des Moines trying to pay my bills and afford my drinking habit. I worked as a receptionist at a car dealership, I sold furniture, was a restaurant manager, and I worked in a lot of bars and restaurants. On my nights off, I sat at those same bars and restaurants and drank my memories away. I was looking to forget everything that had happened, while hoping to find self-love at the bottom of those glasses. I dated here and there, some really nice guys, even. But most of them were caught in the same loop I was in: work, drink, repeat.

I even dated a guy we nicknamed Ball Hair. He was in my phone as Ball Hair, and I dated him for over a year.

Ball Hair. Seriously. But the joke of his nickname covered up something darker.

Ball Hair's real name was Ryan. We met at a bar (*shocking, I know*) on St. Patrick's day. He asked a friend of mine if he could have her Mardi Gras beads and she said, "only if you show me your balls!" She was joking, but he showed her anyway. And we lived happily ever after.

Maybe not. But we dated for a few months before we moved in together. We lived in a beautiful apartment on the second floor above a dentist's office close to downtown. This apartment had light wood floors, an open floor plan, and huge windows on three sides that let in a tremendous amount of light. I wish I could have appreciated it more, but we spent so many of our days hungover that the rays of sunshine were usually wasted on us.

Ryan and I had *a lot* of fun together, maybe because we were both broken, but we had such a great sense of humor about it. I would joke about how he was more broken than I was, and he would say the same thing about me, which is probably what made us work.

Having the same hobbies is nice when you're dating, if that hobby is bowling or tennis. When your hobby is bellying up to the bar and stumbling home drunk every night, which was our hobby, things are not as nice.

We were each the victims of our own tragedies. Some nights we would dwell on them, other nights we would ignore them and try to have some fun. We could never predict what kind of night either of us would have, and our moods didn't always coincide.

Those nights in particular were toxic, sometimes even scary.

One night, Ryan and I were at a party at a friend's house. I was in the mood to ignore all of my problems and have a good time. I spent the evening laughing and telling stories, most likely on repeat and at full volume. But Ryan had an edge about him. He was a little too quick with a negative comment and a little too sharp with his friends, and drinking faster than anyone else in the room.

When he started getting nasty with people, I saw the writing on the wall and said goodbye for both of us. I gently coaxed Ryan to the car so we could head home for the night. We were not on the same page, as he wanted to keep the night going, convinced he was still having fun. Thankfully, he got in the car without too much of a fight.

As I drove us home, he complained loudly about having to leave early, eventually convincing himself that I had embarrassed him and had ruined the night. He got himself so twisted while painting this inaccurate picture of the events that he suddenly reached over, grabbed the steering wheel of the Jeep Liberty I was driving, and yanked it toward him angrily. We jerked toward the edge of the highway, rocking side-to-side, as I slammed on the brakes and tried desperately to pry his hands off the wheel.

Thankfully, there were no cars around us as we wrestled for control across three lanes, decelerating from a full sixty-five miles an hour. When I finally managed to pull over, I started crying hysterically. He let go of the wheel, muttered something about how I needed to calm down, and begrudgingly let me drive us the rest of the way home.

The next day, he didn't even remember doing it.

We weren't together much longer after that night. I remember telling my friends about the ride home as they looked at me, horrified. I told them how he reacted, how much we were drinking, and how I knew that it wasn't okay. "But we have so much fun together" I explained. I loved him, and loved who I was when we were "good."

My friend said something that slapped me into reality, leading me to breaking it off with Ryan within the week. She said to me, "You are having fun with him because YOU are fun. He isn't the reason the relationship is good when it is. You are." It was a shock to my system to see myself in that way through someone else's eyes. I have carried an insecurity about myself my whole life, or maybe only ever since that wicked phone call back in the sixth grade. I had a difficult time believing I mattered. To hear it that way gave me the strength I needed to end that relationship.

Ryan had lost his mother before we started dating. She had died following a long battle with cancer. They had been really close, and he never really regained his footing after that. A few years after we broke up he also died. He had moved to Kentucky to be closer to his father and one day he was drinking at a bar and was viciously assaulted. It breaks my heart that he never found his own way forward or healed from his wounds. I pray that Ryan is finally at peace, with his mother by his side.

After Ryan and I broke up, I stayed single for a while. And by single, I mean nothing lasted more than a night.

I was still drinking too much, still looking for something I couldn't name. I needed a reset. A break from the loop I was still stuck in.

Around that time, I had settled a lawsuit with the hospital where I had fought the meningitis. It turns out they made several mistakes that, had they been caught, could have saved me from losing my fingers. The settlement bought me a cute little yellow house and a yellow Jeep Wrangler with a soft top, with enough money left over to travel.

I don't remember deciding to go on a cruise, or even ever wanting to go on one, but lo and behold, I found myself island hopping on the Carnival Valor. I brought my best friend, Shawna, with me. She was a single mother who worked her ass off for her daughter, and it would be years before she could afford a trip like this. Also, I wasn't going to travel alone, and I had plenty of money, so I booked the trip for both of us.

We went in January, because January in Iowa is the absolute worst. It's cold and bleak, and besides sitting at the bar every night, what else was I really doing? We flew into Miami, and then sailed to Nassau, St. Thomas, and St. Maarten on what was essentially a floating city.

What could be better? A bar at sea that stops at beautiful islands? Perfect.

The first night we walked into the main dining room for dinner, and that was a moment I don't think I'll ever forget. The room was incredible. I never use this word, but it was fucking *magnificent*! Every detail was ornate. Gold and crystal chandeliers, crisp white linens, fluted glasses and tufted chairs. I was a long way from the hand me down furniture, and borrowed rooms of my youth.

The food was just as amazing as the room. Like nothing I'd ever had before. Escargot, and fresh lobster, sushi, and exquisite desserts. Who in the world did I think I was, sitting in a room like that? I felt like royalty.

At the table next to us was a large family, all adults, including two guys who looked about our age. As Shawna and I got up to leave, the two guys from that table stood up and introduced themselves.

Rob the first to speak. He was about five feet eight, with long curly hair and an animated way of speaking—always gesturing, always loud. Rick was his opposite. Six foot two, broad-shouldered, quiet. He had short dark hair and glasses, wearing a knit hat with a puka shell necklace. His collared shirt was tucked in with a big belt buckle, sweatbands on his wrists. It was a very specific look—very New York, very Rick—something I'd never seen in the Midwest.

They were headed to the ship's pub crawl and invited us along. I wasn't about to latch onto some guy on the first night, so I brushed it off with a "maybe we'll see you there."

Sure enough, later that night, we ran into them in the dance club. We danced, we laughed, had a few more drinks, and ended up talking on the Lido deck until the early morning. It had rained while we were in the club and there were little pools of rainwater on every chair. Rick wiped off a wet chair with his hand before offering it to me, right before he leaned in and kissed me for the first time.

Rick was never the loudest guy in the room, but he's always been the smartest. And if you're listening, he will have you laughing non-stop. But more than that, he was steady. He didn't drink like I did. He didn't need chaos to feel alive. His quiet confidence made me feel safe.

Rick lived in New York, and I still lived in Iowa, but I still had money and was reckless with it. So, I bought a lot of plane tickets. I flew out to see him and flew him out to see me every couple of weeks. When we were apart, we built our relationship over very long phone calls.

We dated long distance from January through August that year. Every phone call stretched for hours. Every visit felt too short. And by summer, I realized something: I didn't want to keep saying goodbye to him.

So in one of the most impulsive decisions I'd made since leaving California eight years before—since I'd gotten married in Vegas, since I'd booked that first cruise—I did the most on-brand thing possible: I packed up my life and moved to New York.

I sold the yellow house, said goodbye to Iowa, to the bars, to the friends I'd made, to the version of myself who thought she was only worth a phone call past midnight.

The Same Room,
Different Address

Relocating to New York felt exactly the same as moving to Iowa, except I was driving my own car and I had a little money in the bank. But I was still running toward hope, and attempting to run away from myself.

In Des Moines, I had fallen into the same patterns I had built in California: drinking as a hobby, not building a future that was going to sustain me, and generally looking for love in all the wrong places.

I believed I had worn out Iowa, so to speak, and there was no growth left there for me. Similar to a goldfish that can only grow to the size of their bowl, I could only be as successful as the reputation I had built for myself.

And my reputation? Let's just say it wasn't winning me any awards.

But in New York? New York was brand new, another clean slate.

I only knew Rick and his family. I hadn't embarrassed myself in front of anyone there. Nobody knew what a fucking mess I had been, and I could actually be someone amazing in New York. I could be someone new—someone better. Someone who had her shit together.

I decided I was going to go to college in New York. Hofstra, of all places. I applied, and was actually accepted. I was going to study economics because I remembered enjoying that class in high school, and I had nothing else pulling me in any clear direction. I had no idea what I would do with an economics degree; I just felt like that was at least some kind of a plan.

I packed up all of my belongings from my little yellow house, sold my little yellow Jeep, and hit the road east in the Acura I had purchased with the lawsuit money. I drove for two days, spending one night at a roadside hotel in Ohio. The whole drive, I felt like I was shedding my old life with every mile marker.

California April—gone. Iowa April—gone.

I was going to be New York April now, and she was going places. Big places.

I still remember sitting in traffic on the George Washington Bridge with a full bladder, realizing I was in the E-ZPass lane and I did not have an E-ZPass.

Shit.

In a split-second decision, I decided I was a New Yorker now, and I squeezed my way over two lanes to the cash lane as people honked. I never looked back at the girl from California by way of Iowa.

This was my fresh start.

Except it totally wasn't. Because driving over a bridge actually changes nothing.

The first year in New York was harder than I wanted to admit. I made some casual friends at my part-time job selling mortgages, but nothing that would last. I was older than the young college students at Hofstra, so I didn't connect with anyone there either. I finished one semester and it seemed silly to spend all that money on an expensive university when I had no real plans for what I wanted to do with my life.

So, I dropped out.

Rick and I had our ups and downs. We were figuring each other out in real-time, in real proximity, and it wasn't always smooth. I'd pick fights when I was drinking. He'd shut down when things got too intense. We'd break up, then get back together a week later.

I kept waiting for him to realize I wasn't worth the trouble.

His family didn't trust the crazy girl who moved halfway across the country for him. They thought I was straight-up trouble. And honestly? They weren't wrong to be cautious. I was still drinking like it was my second job. I was still the girl who made impulsive decisions and didn't think about consequences.

At Thanksgiving that first year, I got too drunk at his aunt's house and said something I shouldn't have. I don't even remember what it was. But I remember the look on his mother's face. The way the room went quiet. The way Rick drove me home in silence.

I cried the rest of the night, convinced he was going to break up with me. That his family was right about me. That I'd ruined everything.

But he didn't leave.

It was years before I got close to Rick's family. Years before they saw me as more than the impulsive girl who showed up with a car full of my belongings, and no plan.

Years before I stopped proving their suspicions right every time I fucked up.

I thought they needed to believe I was worth trusting, that they needed to stop judging me for my mistakes.

But really? I just needed to stop being so goddamn insecure. Here's what I still didn't understand: You cannot outrun yourself.

I thought a new place, new people and a new chance would somehow make me new. But I wasn't new. I was still me—still drinking too much, still afraid I wasn't enough, still convinced that the next version of myself would be the one that worked.

But the location was never the problem.

The problem was that I kept moving before I ever unpacked my shit. My deep-rooted, emotional shit.

Still, New York gave me something California and Iowa couldn't: *Rick*.

And Rick gave me something I never had before: someone who could see me through the mess. He didn't try to fix me. He didn't demand I be someone I wasn't. He just kept showing up, even when I gave him every reason not to.

Even when his family warned him.

Even when I was still figuring out how to stop running.

Even when I didn't know if I'd ever feel like I belonged anywhere. He stayed.

And slowly—so slowly I didn't even notice it happening—New York started to feel less like a place I was running to and more like a place I could actually stay.

Not because the city changed.

Because I finally stopped trying to outrun myself long enough to let someone catch me.

The Room I Built
with Him

Rick and I dated for another year before we moved in together. I tried to learn from the mistakes I made with Tom and did my best not to challenge his love for me. He made me feel safe, and appreciated. And unlike anyone before him, he showed me through his actions, not just his words.

Early in our relationship, Rick's parents had a vacation home in the Poconos, Pennsylvania. We decided we would spend some time together at their house and learn to snowboard. We went shopping and bought everything we would need: snowboards, boots, bindings, pants, jackets, pads for our hips, gloves, goggles, and a cute little backpack for me. Sure, we could have rented, but I still had some money, so our attitude was: treat yo'self.

That night we slept at his place, and he brought me home early the next morning. Like 4am early. All of our new equipment was in his truck and without a thought, he climbed out and carried everything in and told me to head in and get some rest. It may not seem like much, but it was kind. And it was natural for him, not a big show. That's when I started to see it—this was different. He was different.

One of our favorite things became cooking together. We love to throw a dinner party. It's always a good excuse to learn new recipes, try new foods, and spend quality time with people we love. From our first apartment to our first house, we have planned dozens of elaborate dinners: multiple courses, themed meals, and a perfectly decorated table. No matter what space we're in, we have always moved gracefully in a kitchen together. Like a choreographed dance, we chop, dice, prep, pour, and laugh together for an entire day, making everything perfect for whoever will be joining us at our table.

What's funny about how we do this is that when we met, I could not cook for anything. My meals consisted of Taco Bell, Betty Crocker au gratin potatoes, or premade raviolis with jarred sauce. I could boil water, and I could drive through. But that was the extent of it. In the kitchen with Rick, though, I learned to make elaborate meals and build a skill I desperately needed. This is a tradition I hope we carry into old age.

One of our favorite memories was our first New Year's Eve together. It was late afternoon and we had no plans for how we would celebrate. We hopped on the internet hoping to find something fun to do, or somewhere where we could go last minute. We stumbled across the website for Medieval Times in New Jersey. We both laughed, looked at each other and then I said, "Oh my god, let's do it."

We booked our seats right then, threw some things in an overnight bag, and hit the road toward Jersey. It's still one of my favorite nights. We watched jousting and sword fights and drank ye old Jägermeister shots while eating chicken with our bare hands. We were too drunk to drive home to Long Island, so we found a random hotel with availability and spent the rest of the night in a local dive bar singing along to the jukebox and having the time of our lives.

Those spontaneous adventures became our pattern—we were good at fun, good at laughter, good at living in the moment. But like any young couple learning to build a life together, we weren't perfect.

We had our struggles like any young couple learning to live in a space together. Nothing tragic, and nothing we couldn't work through—just the real-life, day-to-day challenges of building a life together.

We didn't know at the time that my drinking was a real problem because we were in our twenties, and it seemed like everyone was drinking like I was. Or at least that's how it looked to me. I would overdo it some nights, but occasionally so would he. We would spend lazy Sundays hungover watching movies and it was usually not a real issue.

My life was looking stable, but stable in a way that didn't make me want to run for the hills. I had found a place where I could be myself, even on my bad days, and not feel like I would be left behind.

Rick knew that Christmas is special to me, and I had told him the story about my brother's cardiac arrest and the decorated palm tree. So, the week before our first Christmas together as a couple, we went to the tree farm and bought a real Christmas tree for his parents' big Christmas Eve party, and we decorated it together.

The next year, we continued the tradition. It was December 23rd, 2007, the night before the family Christmas Eve party. We went to Rick's parents' house to decorate the tree we had picked out, and delivered the day before. Thinking it was going to be just us, I was in raggedy old black yoga pants and an oversized T-shirt I had stolen from Rick, my hair piled in frizzy curls on top of my head. When his sisters, brother-in-law, and grandmother all arrived unexpectedly for dinner, I was surprised and a little embarrassed.

I left them all in the kitchen while they planned what we would order from the local Chinese restaurant, and I went to decorate the tree in the living room. I hung as many lights as I could squeeze onto the branches and I carefully unwrapped each of the sentimental family ornaments and placed them gently on the tree. I loved that his mother had kept every ornament from Rick and his sisters' childhood. My own ornaments had all been damaged or thrown out before I left California.

There was a fire in the fireplace, and I sang along to classic Christmas songs, bopping my head with the music. I was facing the tree, placing an ornament, when Rick came up behind me, wrapped me in his arms and nuzzled into my neck. His hands were in front of me.

He was holding a ring.

Almost two years after we met, Rick asked me to marry him.

I squealed, "Are you joking right now?!" Followed by, "Yes, of course, yes!"

I stood there in his arms, staring at the ring, tears streaming down my face. His whole family was in the kitchen waiting. He had planned this. They all knew. And he'd chosen me: frizzy hair, yoga pants and all.

This wasn't a Vegas chapel with strangers as witnesses. This wasn't a secret we had to keep. This was his family, waiting in the next room to celebrate our engagement.

This was real.

The next night was Christmas. As we opened presents together with his family, his mother handed me a box. Pulling off the wrapping I saw a Hallmark box and burst into tears. It was a Chinese food container ornament with a fortune cookie attached to it. When you pull the fortune from the cookie, the ribbon says, "What good fortune to have each other."

It was our very first ornament. A tradition that started that night and continues to this day. We have ornaments from every special event, milestone, and vacation. And every year when we unwrap each one and hang it on our own tree, I am transported back to the night when he asked if he and I could be a family.

A few nights before our wedding, as he sat on the top step of the stairs in our apartment, looking down at me on the couch, I said to him, "You know, Rick, I think you see me. You see something inside me that I don't. You knew I could be a wife, and one day, hopefully a mother, even though when we met, I only saw myself as a mess. You saw more, and nobody else ever has."

He just grinned and said, "Yeah, I know. I'm pretty great." He always makes me laugh.

I didn't grow up with a healthy husband-and-wife example to learn from. My mom and stepfather's relationship was toxic, and I knew enough to know I didn't want that. I had glimpses of healthy love through my grandparents, my best friends' parents, and a few others. It was because of those glimpses, I knew marriage could be better than the example I had been given. I didn't know how or when I would find it, or if I would at all. But I knew I wouldn't settle for less.

Rick has been patient, loving, and hilarious since day one. He finds a way to make me laugh, even in my hardest moments. He doesn't push me to be someone I'm not, but he makes me want to be a better me. When I imagined what my life could look like as an adult, I couldn't have dreamed up half of what I have with Rick.

We got married in April of 2009. It was a beautiful day, mid-seventies, with a perfect blue sky and wispy clouds.

Planning that wedding felt nothing like the rushed, secret weddings with Tom. This time, I got to choose everything: my dress, the flowers, the music, the guests. I got to stand up in front of everyone we love and say "I do" without shame, without secrecy, without wondering if I was making a mistake.

This time, I was sure.

We danced our first dance to La Vie en Rose while 175 people who loved us looked on. We had built an incredible community of family and friends together, they were all there to celebrate with us.

What a stark contrast to that tiny chapel in Las Vegas and Minneapolis, surrounded by strangers.

We honeymooned for ten beautiful days in St. Lucia. Naps on the beach, massages, champagne, and not a single mirror on the ceiling.

For the first time in my life, I wasn't running toward something or away from something. I was simply walking forward with a man who had chosen me, all of me... missing fingers and broken pieces included.

The Room I Built
for Bella

Rick knew I was pregnant before I did.

I was exhausted and weepy about everything (*or nothing, depending on your perspective*). When I cried because he was leaving for work and I would "miss him so much," he gave me an exasperated look and said, "You are so pregnant."

What a man thing to say. As if I could only miss him if I were overrun by hormones. That's so annoying.

Sure, it happened to be true, but it was still really annoying.

Rick's family looks very different from mine. His dad is one of seven siblings; his mom one of five. He's the middle child with two sisters. Now that we were married, his big, loud, Spanish-Irish family was my family, too. That's a bit overwhelming, considering I could count all the members of my family on my two hands. Post-amputation.

Too dark? Maybe. *True*? Absolutely.

I loved the thought of bringing a baby, our baby, into that family. His or her life would look so different from mine, and I hoped and prayed it would be a good thing.

My mother-in-law, who worked as an ultrasound tech, offered to scan the baby and tell us the gender. I didn't see that as necessary; I was certain it was a boy. His name would be Jack Richard Garcia. Jack, after my grandfather and Richard, after his father. It was a strong, masculine name. I hoped he would carry it with all the pride I had when I gave it to him.

Then Rick's mother, with the wand to my belly, smiled and said, "It's a girl."

Well, I thought, she's obviously terrible at her job, because that could not be right.

We thanked her, and they celebrated as I quietly wiped the jelly off of my round little belly. Then Rick and I left the room where my life had just changed forever, but not in the way I had pictured. We climbed into my red Grand Cherokee, the "grocery getter" I had bought the week we found out I was pregnant, and I cried. Not happy tears. But the kind that come when something inside of you breaks open.

Rick, always the fixer, decided the best way to handle my emotional breakdown was a trip to Babies "R" Us.

"You'll feel better if you can find something for her," he said, like buying one tiny pink dress would erase the dread I carried. It was a testament to how little he understood about my relationship with my mother.

But, he tried.

When he saw the tears in my eyes at every ruffle, bow, and pink blanket, he quietly grabbed me a bag of M&M's. He had grown up with sisters and knew enough that if shopping couldn't fix it, maybe chocolate could.

Isn't he the cutest?

I hated everything in that store. Maybe it was rebellion against the news, or maybe it was the denial that still clung to me. But I knew one thing: I would eventually have to decorate the room this little girl would live in. Thankfully, I found a compromise: a ladybug motif. Mint, ivory, red and black. Stronger. Cleaner. Not pink. It wasn't about rejecting this baby girl. It was about finding a way into this new path that allowed me to breathe.

From that day until the delivery, I carried a heavy denial deep in my gut. I convinced myself that maybe Rick's mom had been wrong, and every ultrasound technician that followed was wrong. That, at birth, someone would announce, "It's a boy!" and I could finally exhale in relief.

I know how this sounds, and I know this might be hard to understand if you had a good mother. But when the only mother-daughter relationship you know is broken, the thought of recreating it is terrifying.

I did not trust myself to raise a daughter. A son I could understand. My brother Chris taught me that I was capable of creating a bond with a little boy. Daughters felt foreign, unreachable, like I would need to speak a language I had never been taught.

How could this little girl ever love me? How could I love her, when my own mother-daughter bond was jagged and broken?

Anxiety overwhelmed every ultrasound, every doctor appointment, and every conversation about her name, her nursery, our excitement.

And yet, she came.

She came early, when I was only thirty-three weeks pregnant. I'll spare you the gory details, to refrain from writing a medical journal. Just know this: she was so tiny, her delivery was dramatic and scary, but she was perfect.

She wasn't breathing when she was born, and the whole room fell silent. Nurses and doctors rushed to her, and whatever they did in the corner of that room, it saved her life. For just a moment, I heard her cry. They intubated her to help her breathe and brought her to me so I could see my daughter for the first time. She was so small and had a tube coming out of her mouth. Still, but awake. Her tiny hand curled into a fist no bigger than a walnut.

She was my beautiful little girl.

I don't know what I was so afraid of. I could absolutely love this girl, with everything I have, for as long as I have it.

The years between that hospital room and now have been filled with moments I never knew I could have. First steps. First words. Bedtime stories and scraped knees and birthday parties. All the ordinary, extraordinary moments of watching her become herself.

My daughter, Bella, is a teenager now. I'm doing alright, thanks for asking. She is the most beautiful soul I've ever met. I don't take all the credit for her strength or her kindness; some of that is just who she is. But some of it is in how she was raised. I didn't give her a childhood she needed to survive. I gave her one she could simply enjoy.

We raised her to be a helper, to apologize without excuse when she's wrong, to see needs and fill them. She clears tables without being asked. She raises money for senior cats. She started a mindfulness project at her school because, as she tells it, "Most of these kids don't have moms like you. They need help with their mental health and don't know how to find it."

Hearing that makes me wonder: *Who would I have been if I had been raised by that couple in Lake Tahoe?*

The rooms my daughter occupies are brighter because she's in them. Even on the hardest days of being a mother, there is still so much joy. I will never understand how my mother didn't get that, and honestly? It makes me sad for her. She missed out on so much because she just couldn't see it.

But I'll be damned if that will be the story about me and my daughter. I am not my mother. And Bella isn't me.

We get to write our own story, 3,000 miles away from where mine was written. But it might as well be a different universe.

We're building rooms where her laugh melts my heart, where she calls me her emotional support mom. Just writing that makes my breath catch in my throat. My teenage daughter, the one I was so afraid to have, said that to me.

This is part of my castle that I got to build, and will keep building, and it's filled with light and love.

One day, if my daughter is sitting in a room with a sonogram wand pressed to her little round belly, I hope she is nothing but excited to hear the words, "It's a girl."

But first, she'll have to grow up. And growing up, I would learn, comes with its own rooms—ones I couldn't predict, couldn't control, and couldn't protect her from, no matter how hard I tried.

The Room Where
I'm The Mom

The little girl I was so afraid to have did grow up. She grew into someone beautiful and kind and funny. She became my favorite person; proof that I could love a daughter and be loved by one in return.

But she also grew into someone who struggles. Watching my daughter fight anxiety and ADHD hurts my soul in ways I didn't expect. And I can't help but wonder if every decision I made while raising her has led her to have these overwhelming feelings.

Did I push her too hard? Were there too many rules? Is she scattered because I'm scattered?

I see all the missed opportunities—the times I yelled when she needed kindness, the times she wanted to play, and I was "too busy."

From a young age, Bella has had panic attacks. I wish I knew then what was happening because they mostly looked like temper tantrums. Usually, these attacks would start when she was doing her homework or cleaning her room, when she had some kind of responsibility. I could see her getting wound up: her breath would catch, her eyes would fill with tears, her small hands in tight little fists. And then she would start to repeat herself. Over and over again. She would perseverate on one phrase through the entire panic attack.

I didn't know this was a thing with panic attacks, so I would get mad and reprimand her.

"Stop saying that," I'd snap, with my own anxiety rising to meet hers. "Just stop."

But she couldn't stop. And I couldn't see what was really happening, that my daughter was drowning right in front of me, and I was telling her to swim harder.

I thought I was teaching her resilience. I thought I was preparing her for a world that wouldn't coddle her feelings. I thought I was being a good mother.

I was wrong.

The guilt of those moments sits heavily in my chest. I replay them at night sometimes—her small face twisted in panic, my voice sharp with frustration.

But I can't go back. All I can do is show up differently now. And understanding why I struggled for so long has helped me show up better.

When I was diagnosed with ADHD at forty-six , it cracked something open in me. Suddenly, all those years of feeling like a failure had a name. The forgotten appointments. The messy house. The bills paid late. The constant sense that I was drowning in my own life.

It wasn't laziness. It was my brain, working against itself. And then, Bella was diagnosed, too.

I sat in the psychologist's office while he explained how ADHD can present as depression and anxiety in girls, and all I could think was: Oh my God. I gave this to her.

The psychologist must have seen it on my face because he stopped mid-sentence. "This isn't your fault. And it's not a death sentence. It's just information."

Just information. As if this information doesn't change everything.

But he was right. Because knowing what Bella was dealing with meant I could finally help her in ways no one had ever helped me.

The panic attacks look different now. Not because they've stopped. Bella still gets overwhelmed, still spirals when the homework seems impossible or her room feels like chaos she can't control. But I look different.

Now, when I see her breath catch, I don't tell her to stop. I sit down next to her.

"What does it feel like?" I ask.

Last week, she was trying to write an essay for English class. I watched her hands ball into fists, watched her breath get shallow.

"I can't do this," she said. "I can't do this, I can't do this, I can't do this."

I sat down on the floor next to her chair. I didn't touch her. Sometimes touch makes it worse. I just sat there.

She kept repeating the phrase. I kept sitting. After a few minutes, her breathing slowed. After a few more, she looked at me.

"Can you help me outline it?" she asked. "Of course," I said.

And we did. Together.

Sometimes she can't answer. Sometimes all she can do is repeat the same phrase, and I let her. I don't interrupt. I don't correct. I just stay.

"You're okay," I tell her, once she's calmer. "Your brain is scared, but you're safe. We're going to get through this together."

And we do. Every single time. We do.

I've learned that the best apology isn't words, it's change. I can't take back the times I yelled when she needed kindness. I can't undo the moments I was too busy, too tired, too wrapped up in my own anxiety to see hers. But I can show her that people can grow. That mothers can learn. That healing is possible, even in the middle of the mess.

Sobriety changed me as a mother. Not just because I finally stopped scaring her with my chaos, but because drinking kept me numb. It kept me reactive. It kept me from being fully present.

I was always half-somewhere else, managing my own chaos, trying to keep my head above water.

Being sober, I can breathe. I can pause before I react. I can see her panic for what it is, instead of taking it personally; instead of feeling like her struggle is proof of my failure.

Therapy helped, too. I've been unpacking my own childhood, my own trauma, my own triggers. And the more I heal, the less of that I pass on to her. I used to think my anxiety was just part of who I am, proof that I'm broken, that I'll always be broken. But now I see it differently. My anxiety is information. It tells me when I'm overwhelmed, when I need to slow down, when I'm trying to control things I cannot control. And now I teach Bella that, too.

"Your brain is trying to protect you," I tell her when she's spiraling. "It's just doing its job a little too loudly right now."

She's starting to believe me. I can see it in the way she talks about herself, less shame, more curiosity. Less *what's wrong with me?* and more *my brain works differently.*

That shift—that's everything.

And she has something else I never had: a village. I'm fortunate to raise Bella in a big family. Rick and I are very close to his parents and his sisters. No relationship is perfect—we've had our ups and downs—but you hear horror stories about in-laws and I am so grateful for the family I married into.

Rick's family is more traditional than mine—his parents have been married forty-five years and counting. They know what it means to show up, even when it's hard. They know what it means to love someone through their worst days, and celebrate them on their good days.

Bella has grandparents who adore her. She has aunts who text her memes and take her shopping. She has cousins who make her laugh until she cries. She has the village I never had.

And when I watch her with them, confident, goofy, wholly herself, I think:

This is what breaking the cycle looks like.

Not perfect. Not polished. Just different.

My real job isn't to be a perfect mother. It's to give Bella a healed mother. Or at least a mother who's healing—who's willing to look at her own shit, to apologize when she gets it wrong, and to keep showing up even when it's hard.

She trusts me. Because she knows I get it. She knows I've been where she is: scared, overwhelmed, convinced that something is fundamentally wrong with her.

And she knows I made it through. Messy, imperfect, and still learning—but through.

If I can show her that, maybe she won't spend forty-six years thinking she's broken before someone finally gives her the manual to her own brain. Maybe she'll know sooner than I did that different doesn't mean damaged. Maybe she'll build rooms for herself that are full of light from the start, instead of spending decades trying to find the switch.

There are still hard days. Days when I snap at her because I'm tired, when I'm too wrapped up in my own struggles to see hers, when I feel like I'm failing her all over again.

But the difference now is that I don't stay there. I apologize. I explain. I tell her, "I got that wrong, and I'm sorry. Let's try again."

And we do.

I'm not the mother I wished I could be. But I'm becoming the mother she needs.

And that, I'm learning, is enough.

The Room Where
He Stays

In March 2020, I had COVID. Original-flavor COVID. Remember when they were building tents in hospital parking lots? I was watching from inside the hospital. It was intensely scary.

One night, I was in pretty bad shape. They couldn't get my fever under control, and it just kept rising: 102, 103, 103.5. They brought in an ice blanket, which still makes me want to cry just thinking about it. The nurse, unsure how to help me, had tears in her eyes when she said, "I do not want to send you to the ICU. I just can't."

It was three o'clock in the morning, my third night in that room. I was alone, and the door was closed, but I could hear the announcements for each code blue and rapid response in the hospital. I could hear people rushing past my door, yelling orders, trying to save as many people as they could from this illness they knew nothing about.

They put me on a mat filled with ice water, then packed ice between my legs, under my armpits, and behind my neck. I lay there in just a tank top and underwear with only a thin sheet covering me, shivering so violently I thought my bones would crack. On oxygen and still struggling to breathe. Exhausted. My whole body sore from it all.

I was so afraid, and I was alone. And the meningitis from almost twenty years earlier was haunting my thoughts.

So, I called Rick. He answered on the second ring, his voice groggy with sleep.

"Hey, babe. You okay?"

Tears were running down my face and I could barely speak without my teeth chattering. "I'm s-so c-cold."

Within five minutes, he had me laughing. I don't even remember what he said. But he brought me out of that room in the hospital and into a room where it was just us. Just him making me laugh and making me feel safe.

That's who he is to me. It doesn't matter where I am in the world or what I'm experiencing; he is my phone call. He grounds me.

I love you, Rick.

And yet, there's still a piece of me, shaped by my mother's voice, that whispers he could do better. He could find a wife who keeps a spotless house, cooks incredible dinners, and stocks the fridge with his favorite meals.

I am the wife who forgets what he asked me to pick up at the store. Who doesn't see laundry piles when I get hyper-focused on new hobbies. We throw out too much food and order takeout because I never plan ahead for dinner. I'm chronically tired and fifty pounds heavier than I was five years ago.

He could do better. But he doesn't.

He does me.

Recently, I needed an unexpected surgery. I was frustrated, but not too worried, as this would be my fifth pelvic surgery. While waiting in pre-op, my blood pressure kept climbing. The nurse was checking it every ten minutes, and every time, it was higher than the time before. She needed a number that wasn't too high to clear me, so we just kept trying while I silently prayed we wouldn't have to reschedule.

On what was probably the seventh attempt, Rick looked at me and said, sternly, "That's enough! Get it together and knock it off with this!"

To anyone else, it probably sounded like he was actually angry, but I knew better. He was joking, but now I had to lie perfectly still trying not to laugh. He honestly thought that yelling at me would lower my blood pressure.

Welp, in this worst-case scenario, it fucking worked. My pressure dropped. I got cleared for surgery.

And now? Every time he annoys me, he tells me he's helping. That it's medically proven and documented that he lowers my blood pressure.

I am so screwed.

That's the thing about a love like ours. It sneaks up on you in the middle of panic, or pre-op, or a bad joke that lands exactly where it needs to.

He doesn't heal me by fixing anything. He heals me by staying. He's the proof that love can be steady, even when I'm not. And every time he makes me laugh when I should be crying, I realize I've been slowly redecorating this room, the one where I learned love could hurt, and I've been filling it with light.

For so long, I carried my parents' rejection like it was proof of my worth. As though their inability to love me meant I was unlovable. But Rick continues to show me otherwise.

One day, I will step back into the room where my father left me behind, and all the rooms where my mother left her scars. I will redecorate them with light and finally lay the darkness where it belongs—on my parents' doorstep, not mine. I will finally believe that what I bring to the table is enough.

And just because they couldn't love me the way I needed them to doesn't mean that my husband can't.

The Room Where I
Wanted Eggs

Rick and I were steadily building a life together. He had joined the
FDNY when we got engaged, and he was loving being a firefighter. I honestly can't think of him doing anything else—the job fits him
perfectly. But I hadn't yet found my calling.

I had been working in technology up until Bella was born. It was
a cool job—I traveled all over the tri-state area training clients on their
new phone and computer systems. It was fun, and I was good at it, but I
knew it wasn't what I was put here to do. I knew I needed more. I needed
to make a difference.

One afternoon, Rick and I were discussing this very thing: what
the hell I was going to do with my life? We started scrolling through the
degree programs at the community college near us, and as soon as I saw
the words, I knew.

Occupational Therapy Assistant.

It was like something clicked into place. All those years of recovery,
of learning to adapt, of refusing to let the limitations of my hands define
me—suddenly it all made sense.

This was the room I was supposed to build.

While I was in school for Occupational Therapy, we had to complete a project where we feigned a disability, and attempted to perform a
daily task to see how hard it could be. My disability would be a non-func-
tioning left arm.

Of course, the morning I started this project, I didn't want something simple, like cereal. I wanted eggs.

Making scrambled eggs with one hand is really, really difficult. Go
ahead and try it—you'll see. Cracking the egg without the shell falling in.
Whisking with a fork while keeping the bowl steady. The butter sizzling

in the pan while you're still trying to get the damn thing beaten. By the time I got those eggs on a plate, they were cold and I was swearing.

The takeaway for that project was how important it is to be able to make choices for ourselves. I wanted eggs; that was my choice. I shouldn't have to want cereal just because it was functionally easier.

That's how I see occupational therapy: it gives people choices. It lets them live the life they want, on their own terms.

That's how I see occupational therapy: it gives people choices. It lets them live the life they want, on their own terms. I learned this lesson firsthand. After my battle with meningitis, I needed both physical and occupational therapy. Following my amputations, I had no grip or coordination with my left hand; the only fingers I had left were my thumb, my pinky, and two-thirds of my ring finger.

How would I tie my shoes? Blow-dry my hair? Draft this book? Everything looked different now, but none of it was impossible.

Unfortunately, the occupational therapist assigned to me back then did not share the same philosophy. He arrived at our first meeting with a book of adaptive equipment: springy shoelaces so I wouldn't have to tie my shoes, a stick to type with so I could punch the keys one at a time.

He told me I couldn't do things the way I used to. He wasn't wrong about that. But he also implied there were things I simply wouldn't be able to do at all.

He didn't see *me*.

I was twenty-two years old—a vibrant, stubborn waitress and bartender who had just been to hell and back. His job was to tell me I could do anything while helping me bridge the gap when I hit a limitation. Don't start me at nothing and hope that I'll settle for crumbs.

I fired him the moment he left. Fuck that guy.

Then I sat on the edge of my bed, alone in that room where someone had just told me to see my life through a lens of limitation and I picked up a pair of drawstring pants. Taking the strings in my remaining fingers, I worked them clumsily until I tied the neatest little bow. Then I did it again. And again. Until it was fast, until it became automatic—just like it had been when I still had ten fingers.

I didn't want cereal. I wanted eggs. And I was going to find a way to make them.

From my very first class in the Occupational Therapy Assistant program, I knew I was in the right room. I sat there taking notes and everything made perfect sense. Function, meaningful occupations for mental health, the building of a person through development.

This was my calling.

I spent two years in the program and graduated at the top of my class. Not because I was the smartest or the most gifted—though I did work my ass off. But I believe it was divine intervention. I was supposed to be there. Everything clicked the second I heard it.

Working in occupational therapy has always been as much for me as it is for the patients I treat. Giving people back their sense of choice allowed what happened to me to make sense. It gave meaning to my meningitis. It gave it purpose.

Because I had been in that bed, because I had fought to recover, I understood the pain and frustration my patients were feeling. I could meet them where they were. And I could guide them through their own living nightmare, lighting the way with my story—and with proof that hope and determination matter.

I still make scrambled eggs with one hand occasionally. These days, they're pretty damn good.

In the end, I realized my calling was simple: to help people want their own "eggs" and to show them that, no matter how impossible it seems, there's always a way to make them. Every time a patient learns to button their shirt, feed themselves, or returns home—that's not just function returning. That's dignity. That's choice. That's eggs.

The Room Where I
Wasn't Alone

There is a part of every room that I carry that I haven't mentioned. Like a piece of furniture you've had for so long that you don't even remember where it came from.

When I was twelve years old, in the sixth grade, my mom, Brian, and I lived in a rented house in Anaheim, California. I had a huge bedroom, where I would make up dance routines to Huey Lewis and the News or The Beach Boys. I was so unbelievably awkward; I wore my mom's hand-me-downs, and I had no idea what to do with my curly hair, so it was frizzy and never once looked nice. I was kind of a mess. I didn't have a single friend at the school I attended, but I wanted one so badly.

I remember vividly walking home from school one afternoon when three girls from my grade approached me. We weren't friends, but I knew who they were. As they came closer and called out my name, I thought: this was it. This was the moment I had been waiting for all year. Finally, someone noticed me, and they wanted to be my friend.

We walked a few blocks together, and I mostly listened to them talk about New Kids on the Block, pretending to know what they were referring to. One of them mentioned she was having the other girls sleep over that night. She said that I should ask my mom if I could come too!

Holy. Shit.

I had finally broken through. I could hardly contain my excitement.

When I got home, I burst through the door, ran to my mom, and begged her to let me go. Laughing and spinning through the kitchen, I told her everything: how this girl had asked me to come, how the others were going to be there, and how I just had to go.

"Yes," she said. Of course I could go.

The girl had written down her phone number for me so, as soon as my mom said yes, I ran to the phone on the wall and called. She answered, and I could hear laughter in the background. "Perfect", I thought. The other girls were already there. I told her my mom had said yes, asked what time I should come. That's when she really laughed. Not the same excited laugh I had moments before. Not the laugh of someone happy to welcome me in. It was darker. Cruel.

"Oh my God!" She said, "We were totally kidding! We don't want you at our sleepover!" and the phone went dead.

I was crushed. Now, not only was I alone, but it was an absolute joke.

Thankfully, I wasn't in that school for much longer. My mom met my stepdad, and not long after that, we moved into his house in Westminster, California.

Another new city. Another new school.

For once, I was looking forward to the change. I couldn't wait to get away from the girls at that school, even though it meant I would be starting over again, this time in January, so the year was already well underway.

It was my first day of sixth grade at Cecil B. DeMille Elementary. My mom had braided my hair into a heart-shaped French braid. I wore a Debbie Gibson T-shirt with a stone-washed, denim, cropped jacket covered in chains and buttons and tight, black shorts. I was the epitome of trying too hard.

During recess, on my very first day, I met Stacey.

I can't tell you exactly what she saw in me that day, but whatever it was, it stuck. From that moment on, she has been part of my story. She has been in every room I've carried since. Sometimes in the background, sometimes front and center, but always there. Like that piece of furniture you don't notice until you stop and realize you can't imagine the room without it.

Stacey has known every version of me, every room, every chapter. Good or bad. She knows about every embarrassing haircut and every boyfriend. The one in high school with layers of plaque on his teeth. The one in my twenties that she is still convinced is gay.

She knew Kevin and Tom. She has known me lost, drunk, the survivor, the wife, and the mother. She has witnessed every renovation of my life's castle, every room I've redecorated or torn apart.

And she stayed.

When she came to see me in the hospital after my amputation, I cried to her about how I wouldn't be able to blow-dry my hair anymore, *of all things.* The room was dark around us, but where I lay in the bed and she sat in the chair leaned toward me, the same glow from the bus station warms the memory. She smiled, with tears filling her eyes, and said, "We will get you the cutest pixie cut *ever.*" Knowing full well I could never pull that off, but also knowing it was exactly what I needed to hear in that moment.

Stacey and I also have a tradition that we laugh about every time we're together: I cannot refuse a dare from her. For thirty-five years, if Stacey dared me, I had to do it. It didn't matter what it was.

"I dare you," she'd say with that grin, and I was done for.

I once had to pretend to bite the fat roll on the back of a stranger's neck at a dance club. She dared me to ask our 6th grade teacher what a douche was, to which the teacher replied, "You're going to have to ask your mother."

And then there was the time Stacey and I were hired to babysit for a family friend, and while there, she dared me to take the family's car for a spin. We were fourteen and neither of us could drive stick shift. We made it about fifteen feet before rolling backward into their driveway. We panicked, managed to park it somewhat close to where it had been, and then smoked all their cigarettes to calm our nerves. It's fine. Everything was fine. (*It was not fine.*

And it hasn't just been dares. She has been the one I have called on my hardest days. When my husband and I had our ugliest fights. When Tom and I filed for divorce. When I was drinking myself into my own great depression. She was with me on the bus station floor, and she was there when I graduated from college at thirty-five. She stood with me at my wedding, and my daughter Bella's middle name is Marie, after her Aunt Stacey Marie. Her family practically adopted me. They called me their 'weekend daughter' and gave me the nickname 'May'. I've always been "May" to her family.

Throughout middle and high school, her Gram would drive us to the beach in the summer and to the ice-skating rink in the winter. When her parents would buy something for Stacey, they would always buy a little extra for May.

When home got too dark and scary, they were my safe haven.

She is proof that love and stability existed in my story all along, even when I overlooked it. Through the laughter, the late-night phone calls, the tears, the inside jokes that still make no sense to anyone but us.

This friendship isn't one pivotal room with a single memory; it's the heart that connects them all. Her presence is woven into the fabric of my life, making every room a little brighter just by being there.

The Cuff

I had a hysterectomy in April of 2025. According to my gynecologist, my uterus was "gross." I'm not sure what the diagnosis code is for yucky, but that's where I was. I don't even mind that he said that, honestly.

Anyone can have a regular uterus; at least mine was funny.

For those of you who don't know, a hysterectomy is when your uterus, and in a lot of cases like mine, the cervix, is removed. Without a uterus, you won't have a period. *Woohoo*!

So, imagine my surprise when a few weeks after the surgery I started my period.

That's a bit dramatic, but there was new bleeding. Because, of course there was.

I saw my doctor, and he made the "well, that's gross" face. I'm starting to wonder if maybe he should have gone into ortho or derm or something less displeasing. What he saw was a hole in what was now essentially my new pelvic floor, the vaginal cuff.

Typically, when this happens, it's less than a centimeter wide. They fix it up with a little silver nitrate, and you go about your life.

Typically.

Mine took that silver nitrate like a snack and wanted more. When I went back in for my checkup four weeks later, the hole was bigger.

Not *that* hole. Don't make it weird.

We scheduled another surgery.

I was so frustrated. Another surgery meant more time off work, more recovery, more pain. I'd already been through one surgery. I just wanted to be done.

Luckily for me, I also had a large cyst on my right ovary, the only structure left standing after my hysterectomy. We could kill two birds with one surgery; the doctor would remove the cyst while also performing what's called a "vaginal cuff repair".

In the weeks before my vaginal cuff repair, I had several appointments: presurgical testing, medical clearance from my primary, my cardiologist, my nephrologist... the whole team. (*Or hole team?*)

It was exhausting. Every appointment meant taking time off work, sitting in another waiting room, explaining my medical history to another stranger. And every single one of them needed to know what procedure I was having.

Which brings me to the phone calls.

I usually made the phone calls for these appointments on my lunch break at work, sitting at my desk with five coworkers' desks lined up next to mine in a corner. We shared everything in our little corner of the rehab gym. Our frustration with our husbands, our sex lives, our hopes and dreams to one day leave this job for something more worthy of our talents...

One thing I didn't want to share was the phrase "vaginal cuff repair."

But for some reason, there isn't a single receptionist or scheduler on the other end of the phone who could hear the words "vaginal cuff repair" without me repeating—and essentially—shouting them. While my coworkers ate their salads or last night's leftovers.

Every fucking time:

"What procedure are you having?" "Vaginal cuff repair."

"Sorry, ma'am, it's a little loud in here. Could you repeat that?"

"VAGINAL CUFF REPAIR!"

Part Four

The Room Before
the Light

In November 2020, I tripped at work and broke my hip. Who breaks their hip at forty-two years old without serious trauma? Apparently I do. My doctor was shocked. But I wasn't. This was the kind of thing that happened to me, just one more weird, unlucky, inexplicable thing amongst a pretty long string of them.

My doctor gave me a set of crutches and told me to keep the weight off of my hip for eight weeks, allowing the bone to heal on its own. It didn't. When the X-rays came back showing no progress, the doctor scheduled me for surgery to have a plate put in my hip.

I had lost my mobility and, along with it, my independence. I was out of work *again*. This wasn't new for me. The summer before COVID my kidney disease had progressed to a point where I needed treatment. My doctor admitted me to the hospital on two occasions where I received infusions of a drug called Rituxan.

For people like me, whose immune systems sometimes attack their own organs, Rituxan can be a lifeline. It doesn't fix anything for good. But it can calm things down and slow the progression of a disease. I had two infusions, two weeks apart, and then we waited to see how my body would react. Thankfully my body responded well to the infusions, and I haven't needed another one since.

Then I had taken three months off to recover from COVID and was starting to feel like I was *always* sick. Always *something*. I couldn't run or hike or do any of the things that used to make me feel like me. Hell, I couldn't even walk.

I was forty-two years old and stuck in a body that kept failing me. I wanted to do so much. I had so many plans. And yet, I was sitting on the couch, watching the world move on without me. I remember thinking: *What happens after the hip heals? Does my eye fall out? Do I start dialysis?*

My family was asleep on the other side of the house. Bella in her room, and Rick in ours. He had kissed my forehead before bed, leaving me watching TV on the couch, wrapped in a blanket of pain and self-loathing that he couldn't see. If he had known what was coming, he never would've left me alone.

Before we move forward I want you to know: I did not want to die. I just needed a fucking minute. Just a minute where my mind wasn't racing, where I wasn't thinking about all the things I couldn't do or all the ways everything had gone wrong. I just wanted one breath that didn't hurt. One moment when I didn't feel like a failure.

Just. One. Fucking. Minute.

But I couldn't see a light at the end of my tunnel. So, I did what I usually did to quiet my racing thoughts. I got drunk.

I started with one drink, just to take the edge off. But the edge didn't go anywhere, so I had another. And another.

The thoughts came faster with every sip. Every overwhelming thought of who I was becoming, and everything I had already been through turned into fuel for the fire I was building inside myself. I hated my body. I hated my weakness. I hated the life I had somehow ended up with.

The voice in my head started shouting louder than the TV.

Why am I like this?

What am I going to be, some disgusting person who just lies around forever? Why would Rick stay married to me when I can't do anything?

He didn't marry this. He should leave and find somebody better.

Bella doesn't need a mom who can't have fun with her. She's always worried about me. She'd be better off without me.

Each thought landed like a punch. *What kind of piece of shit am I? I can't clean my house. I can't cook. I can't take care of my family. I am a burden.*

I couldn't escape the echo of my own disgust. I wanted to stop thinking but I didn't know how. I kept drinking instead, chasing numbness, chasing quiet, chasing anything that wasn't reality.

The end of the night is blurry. I do remember crawling into bed next to Rick. I kissed his cheek, and as he stirred, I whispered, "Babe, I love you. Also I either took all the Xanax or none of it. I'm not sure. Goodnight."

I wasn't trying to be dramatic. I wasn't trying to get attention. I genuinely couldn't remember. The lines between intention and accident had vanished hours ago, swallowed by the fog of exhaustion, alcohol and pain.

As I drifted toward sleep, I heard Rick take a breath, sharp and panicked, and immediately shot out of bed to check the bottle.

I don't remember what happened next.

The Room That
Held Stillness

T he next thing I knew, it was morning.

I woke up in my bed feeling sick. The kind of sick that settles in your bones, telling you you've gone too far. My mouth was dry. My head was pounding.

And I had no memory of what had happened the night before.

I kept my eyes closed, trying to piece it together. I remembered the couch. The TV. The drinks. But after that? Nothing.

The air in our house felt different. I could feel it before I even opened my eyes. It was heavy. Wrong.

You see, I've been drunk before. We'd fought before. I'd been obnoxious, emotional, and embarrassing. And I always knew when I was "in trouble" the next morning, when I'd pushed too far and there would be fallout to manage soon thereafter. But this... this felt different.

I lay still, listening. I could hear Rick pacing in the hallway. His steps were too quick, too deliberate. The floorboards creaked under his weight.

Then I heard my sister-in-law, Julie's voice, low and steady. Rick telling Bella to grab what she needed for the day. The rustle of a backpack. Julie was taking Bella somewhere.

Why?

Their voices were careful and hushed, a back and forth of "thank you" and "I love you," —the sound of people tiptoeing around something fragile. Once the front door closed, the silence that followed cracked something open in my memory.

And just like that, it all came back to me.

Fuck.

Oh my God.

I need help.

Rick came into the bedroom, his eyes red from crying. His voice was calm, too calm as he said, "Get yourself together. You're going to the hospital."

That was fair. Reasonable. I needed help.

The staff in the emergency room were wonderful. They were kind and quietly compassionate in that way only people who've seen everything can be. They took everything I had, including my underwear, and gave me a gown and a gurney. Oh, and they let me keep my crutches.

The crutches were a logistical nightmare for them because, apparently, crutches are considered weapons in the behavioral health unit. And there was a no weapons allowed policy. So even though a person in my condition would typically be admitted into the behavioral health or psychiatric unit, instead, I spent eight long hours in a curtained corner of the ER with a quiet woman assigned to sit beside me and make sure I didn't do anything "crazy."

I wasn't crazy, though. I was just exhausted.

A psychologist came to speak to me and I told her everything. She sat patiently, listening to me vomit all of my trauma onto her. My history with my mother, my illness, the alcohol, the COVID, the hip, and all of the feelings around failure that I carried throughout the years.

She could see that I was overwhelmed and significantly depressed. She called Rick and confirmed that I would be okay to come home, that he felt confident I wouldn't actually hurt myself. She increased my antidepressants and sent me home with instructions to follow up with both my therapist and my doctor.

Bella had spent the day with Julie, blissfully unaware of what had happened. She still doesn't know. Maybe one day I'll tell her, when she's older and strong enough to hold that truth without it shaking her. But for now, she just gets to be a kid who had a fun day with her aunt while her mom got the help she needed.

While lying on that hospital gurney, I realized the last thing I actually wanted was to die. I wanted to live. I wanted to stay in this beautiful, complicated, messy life, even with all its pain, because of the people I love. Because of Rick. Because of Bella. Because of the light I had fought so hard to find.

That emergency room gurney became its own strange room in my house. Not a room of trauma, but a room of stillness.

It was the quiet I had been chasing. Strange, because an emergency room has never been a quiet place. There were alarms, distant voices, carts rolling past, but inside me, for the first time in years, everything stopped. My mind wasn't spinning.

For a few hours, I didn't have to fix anything or prove myself to anyone. I just stared at the chipping blue paint on the walls, the holes in the ceiling tiles, and the curtain between me and the next bed.

I just got to *be*.

That's all I needed. Well, that and an increase in my antidepressants.

That day, I didn't need sleep or distraction. I needed mental quiet. I just wanted the noise to stop. And in that emergency room, it finally did.

I'm so thankful for my husband. For his calm, his understanding of depression, his ability to see my depression for what it was and not to take it personally.

And I will forever be grateful that in my fog that night I went to bed instead of to the medicine cabinet.

In the days and weeks that followed, I began to understand that what had happened that night wasn't just about alcohol, or exhaustion, or even just depression. It was about years of holding my breath. Years of bracing for the next crisis, the next diagnosis, the next time my body would betray me. Every hospital gown, every IV, every sterile ceiling tile had etched a kind of panic into my bones.

Since that night, I have learned how to let myself be held, not just by medication or therapists, but by the people who love me. I learned to stop apologizing for being exhausted, for being human, for needing help.

Healing didn't come in a single moment. It came slowly. But it came.

The Room That
Smelled Like Vodka

I've tried so many things to work through the rooms that held my memories: the one with the pink daybed, the ICU, the chapel in Vegas. I wish I could tell you that one thing worked to heal all of it. But that's not how it works.

Healing isn't linear. It isn't clean. It doesn't arrive in a neat little box with instructions.

Could you imagine, though? That would be really nice.

Healing has looked different for me in every season of my life, and it has required me to return to some rooms more than once. Sometimes kicking and screaming, sometimes crawling, and sometimes with a quiet grace.

But healing doesn't always look like healing at first. Sometimes it looks like survival. And that survival can come with a lot of trial and error.

After my finger amputations, a doctor suggested I try Prozac to help me cope with the trauma. With all the bravado of a stupid twenty-two-year-old and given the stigma I'd absorbed about antidepressants, I refused. I believed taking them meant admitting I was broken and mentally weak. I told myself I could handle it on my own.

Looking back, I wish I'd had the maturity to take the pills and save myself years of pain. But instead, I drank.

I drank for years.

I drank myself into terrible situations and mountains of shame. Because being alone with my thoughts seemed so much worse. I had no skills to process what I'd been through and no tools to sit with my pain. I would replay old rooms over and over until the thoughts got too loud. Then I'd pour myself a drink or head back to the bar.

There was also a kind of camaraderie in those rooms. It wasn't connection necessarily; it was drowning together. I can still smell the bars—the sticky sweetness of spilled liquor on the bar top, the fog of cigarette smoke clinging to my clothes. The bass thumping so loud I could feel it in my chest, drowning out everything I didn't want to hear.

The nights I went out, I could at least disappear into noise, laughter, and oblivion. But the morning always came, and with it shame, apologies, and promises I never intended to keep.

Even after I married Rick, had Bella, and started my OT career, the cycle continued. I told myself I was "better" because I only drank on weekends or at special events. But when I drank, I fucking drank. There was no off switch.

Some nights, I was hilarious; the life of the party. Other nights, I picked fights over nothing. And then there were so many mornings I woke up alone in bed, my husband in another room, my heart heavy with shame.

Something about making the walk of shame in your own home hits differently.

I am grateful I married a man with the patience of a saint, though calling it patience doesn't quite capture what he lived through. He watched me hurt myself and our family for years. He held boundaries when I pushed. And when I was finally ready to get sober, he didn't punish me for the past. He didn't rub my nose in my mistakes or shine a light on every failure. He met me with grace.

I want to say it took too long for me to stop, but it took the time it took. And maybe that's the point: even the worst detours carry lessons.

Those years in the bars were not wasted. They taught me that numbing isn't healing. That drunk isn't joy. And that until I was ready to choose differently, I would keep reliving the same night, over and over, in those same rooms.

Eventually, I'd try other rooms to heal in. Therapy. Medication. Sobriety. But the bar came first, and it taught me the most important lesson: some rooms can't heal you. They can only show you why you need to leave.

The day I finally walked away from that room for good, I didn't feel victorious. I felt exhausted. Scared. And for the first time in years, I felt ready.

The Room I Kept
Dark

T his is the chapter I didn't want to write.

I've mentioned the drinking throughout this story—casually, like it was just part of the scenery. Background noise.

But I haven't told you the worst of it. I've kept this room locked, the lights off, hoping you wouldn't notice the door. But if I'm going to tell my story honestly, I have to open it. I have to let you see what I spent years trying to hide—from Rick, from my daughter, from myself.

So here it is: the stories in the room I kept dark.

It was my sister-in-law's 27th birthday. We had a party in the backyard at Rick's parents' house—that backyard was the scene of so many nights I'm not proud of. This particular night started with me drinking margaritas at three in the afternoon. I say margaritas, but really it was just tequila with enough mix to take the sting off.

Being with Rick's family meant I was never drinking alone, which made it easier to hide my problem. There were at least thirty other people jumping in the pool, dancing, and telling stories at an unnaturally loud volume, all while tipping back drink after drink.

It was getting late and I'd had enough. I was ready to go home. In all my tequila-laced wisdom, I didn't want to interrupt Rick's fun, so I decided I would wait for him to finish his night and then he could take us both home. So, I walked straight through the house—a direct path from the backyard to the front porch—and laid down, curled up on my side, and fell asleep.

In my defense, I really thought this was the perfect solution. He could enjoy his night and pick me up on his way out, like a sloppy party favor. He saw it another way: I passed out on his parents' front porch in full view of his family.

When he did come wake me up to go home, I proceeded to throw up all of my margaritas into his parents' front bushes. A little gift of my own.

Getting home always seemed to be a problem for me. I never wanted the party to end, but when it was time, I would figure out the most inconvenient—or illegal—way out. The illegal part caught up with me eventually.

I used to walk out of parties back in Iowa, and friends had to comb the streets to find me and get me home safely. I would argue and fight to drive home, sometimes sneaking away when I thought no one was looking. By divine intervention, I always made it home.

Except for the night I got arrested.

There was a nightclub I used to frequent in Des Moines called Coconut Joe's. It was exactly how you're picturing it: crowded, full of twenty-somethings listening to "In Da Club" by 50 Cent while drinking kamikazes and vodka Red Bulls.

One night, I thought I was the hero when I saw a girl being pushed around by someone, maybe a boyfriend. I stepped in to "save the day," pretending to know her so he would back off. She seemed genuinely relieved. I sat with her and we hung out for another few drinks, and when it was time to call it a night, he started following her to her car. I told her I would follow her home to make sure she was safe. We all got into our respective cars and now there were three drunk idiots on the road: myself, this girl, and that asshat.

I didn't realize how bad off she was until we hit the highway. She was in front of me and swerving across three lanes, braking and speeding up, and generally just a danger to anyone on the road. Someone must have seen this disaster waiting to happen and called 911. A few minutes later, cops pulled us both over.

I wasn't even embarrassed. I wasn't afraid. It was like I just couldn't see the reality of the situation. I still thought I was being cute. Even when I blew .12 on the breathalyzer and was arrested and charged with driving under the influence I was still laughing. I chatted up the troopers all the way to the station, convinced I had been doing a good thing, and the system just wasn't seeing it correctly. I even offered to buy the troopers a beer if they ever stopped into the bar I worked in.

What the fuck was I thinking?

At the station, the official breathalyzer registered .099—just under the legal limit. The charges were reduced to public intoxication, and I called my friends to come pick me up.

Part of me wishes I'd suffered some actual consequences that night. Maybe I would have changed my behavior sooner? Probably not, though. It still took twenty more years for me to want to change.

Driving drunk was something I did a lot. I carry so much shame for that, but it is part of my story—a dark part, hidden in a room much like Coconut Joe's. I keep the lights out and the music too loud so I don't have to recognize anything specific about those nights.

After I settled the meningitis lawsuit, I was shopping for a new car. A friend who was an Acura salesman let me take a brand new Acura TL—a $50,000 car—for the weekend to test drive it. Feeling like hot shit, I immediately took the car to show it off to my friends.

As it turns out, all of my friends were at the bar. And as I didn't want to be rude, I stayed for a drink. And then I had another. And another. When I woke up the next morning in my apartment, alone, I was so disoriented.

How the fuck did I get here? I thought, trying to piece together the night.

The last thing I remembered was playing pool at one of my favorite little spots. Then the night flashed in a highlight reel—I was having drinks, laughing, and playing pool. All of a sudden bile burned my throat as I remembered; I was playing pool with none other than the guy who had assaulted me.

What in the actual fuck.

I was so desperate to be liked, to be part of the group, to not be excluded, that I was casually socializing with the man who assaulted me months earlier. I spent the day sick to my stomach, dragging myself back and forth to the bathroom, oscillating between throwing up and trying to sleep through one of the worst hangovers I have ever had. And then, several hours into my shame spiral, I remembered the dealership's car.

I shot out of bed in a panic. *Where the fuck was that car?* I ran out to the parking lot frantically looking for the borrowed car...

There it was. Parked in two spots, but safe. Thank God.

I carried shame on so many levels from that night. But even that morning—waking up sick, not remembering how I got home, realizing I'd spent the night with my assailant—wasn't enough to make me stop.

For years, I knew I was out of control. I would make promises periodically, to myself and to Rick that I would try to moderate my alcohol use. Only three drinks... Only on Fridays... Water between each drink... Only beer... No hard liquor...

Years after years of trying to negotiate with my problem. And time after time, I would fail. I would go out with every intention of moderating, and I would wake up alone, Rick sleeping on the couch—away from me—and have to piece together another failed night. I apologized and made promises again and again that I think we both knew I wanted to keep but never would.

I have hundreds of stories like these. Hundreds. These aren't isolated incidents or "that one time I went too far." This was my life. This was every weekend, every holiday, every family gathering, every Tuesday that felt like it needed celebrating.

I wanted to be better. I wanted to stop. I just didn't know how. And I didn't think I could be *me* without it. It took more than twenty more years of embarrassing, dangerous, and shame-filled nights before I stopped drinking.

When I finally got sober, I thought I had escaped the worst of it. I thought I could finally move forward without looking back at all the damage I'd done. Then Bella told me the truth.

After I stopped drinking, my daughter—who was fourteen by the time I got my shit together—told me something that made me feel infinitely smaller than I did in my apartment that morning. She bravely told me that she spent a lot of nights crying herself to sleep when I was drunk. That she was scared when she would see me drunk and out of control.

I was supposed to be her safety. Her guidance. I was supposed to do a better job than my own mother. But with the blurred perspective of an alcoholic, I couldn't even see the damage I was causing.

I thought I was a good mother because I didn't hit her. Because I didn't abandon her. Because I showed up to her school events and made her dinner and tucked her in at night.

But I was still causing damage. Just in my own way.

That's the thing about breaking cycles—you can stop doing the specific harm that was done to you and still find new ways to hurt the people you love most. I didn't give Bella the childhood I had. But I didn't give her the childhood she deserved, either.

And that's a room I'll have to live in for the rest of my life.

Part Five

The Room in the Church Basement

I sat awkwardly in a musty old room on a cold, brown folding chair, picking at the corner of my skin by my thumbnail. It started to bleed, and I wiped it on my jeans while trying to follow along with the story from the "Big Book."

The room was in the basement of a church—how cliché—and it smelled old. Dusty books, stale coffee, damp walls. The air was thick and still. A room full of total strangers, and yet, somehow, we were all living the same moment.

They were reading aloud, like in school, each person taking a few para-graphs before saying "next," and the person beside them would pick it up. Pages rustling. Throats clearing. The creak of folding chairs.

The story was about a woman alcoholic, titled "Women Suffer Too."

I made a joke in my head to avoid the weight of where I was: *Was this ever in doubt? Have you been to a bar, a bachelorette party, a book club, a mom's night out, or a winery in the last twenty years? Women, women everywhere, drinking all there is to drink!*

But the joke didn't land, even in my own mind, because I was one of those women.

It was hard to focus on the story while I was busy counting the people in the room, trying to figure out if I would have to read aloud. *I just fucking got here! I can't do this!* I could feel my heart beating in my throat, and my hands were shaking in my lap.

Thank God the story ended before it reached me, and I could breathe again.

Only then, it got worse. Turns out the reading was the easy part.

I'd seen Alcoholics Anonymous meetings on TV and in movies, and I swear, in reality, it's exactly the same. People introduce themselves by announcing that they are alcoholics. Some of them had been at these meetings for forty years. "Hi, I'm Jenny, and I'm an alcoholic," followed by the resounding "Hi, Jenny." Jenny talks about alcohol and the role it plays in her life. All while heads bob in agreement as I realize that, while we all have different backgrounds, our stories are all the same.

Every story touched my soul, broke my heart, and made me want to run as fast and as far as I could to any other place on Earth.

The thought of speaking and declaring, Hi, I'm April, and I'm an alcoholic...

Wait, what?

The moment I put those words together in my mind—in that phrasing, in that room—my world collapsed just for a moment.

And then, without my consent, tears started running down my face. Not big, ugly sobs. Just quiet, relentless tears, the kind your body lets out when your mind hasn't even caught up yet.

What in the actual fuck was happening?

I could not stop the tears. Like a quiet betrayal, they just kept falling.

Could I just leave? What would I even say if I had to speak?

"Hi, I'm April, and I don't want to call myself an alcoholic, but I'm crying at the thought of it and terrified of saying I'll never drink again. Alcohol has been a huge part of my life for the last twenty-eight years, and it has led me from shameful moment to shameful moment without fail because I have no shutoff switch. One drink equals twelve every time, and then I black out, but I can't seem to find the motivation to stop, even though if I keep going, I could lose everything I care about, including my health and my life. Okay, thanks for listening."

And then what? Do I have to tell people that I'm in AA? Do I have to be an alcoholic forever?

The language felt antiquated. The label felt wrong. *But who was I to judge when I couldn't even get through a holiday without drinking?*

That meeting cracked something open in me. It wasn't about labels, or literature, or whether I'd ever raise a glass of champagne at a wedding again.

It was about facing the truth: alcohol was running my life.

I didn't have to love the room, or the words, or even the process. I just had to decide if I wanted to keep waking up filled with shame or finally learn a different way to live.

August 10th, 2024 was the night I had my last drink.

It wasn't even dramatic. There was no rock-bottom moment, no DUI, no intervention. It was just another night that started with "just one" and ended with me blacking out on someone else's couch.

My coworkers had planned a happy hour at a little restaurant by the water. We had heard that the food was okay, but more importantly, the margaritas were great. Rick was home that night, so he volunteered to drop me off at the restaurant. I would Uber home after a couple of drinks, and we would spend some much-needed romantic time together.

The issue, as usual, was that once I started drinking, I didn't want to eat. So, as soon as that margarita touched my lips, I was doomed.

The next morning, Rick didn't say anything to me. He was asleep in a different room, which meant that whatever I had done had pissed him off enough that he didn't want to be around me. I knew we would have to face my behavior again and how it affected him—the exhaustion, the worry, the wondering how many more times we'd do this dance.

I scrambled through my phone trying to piece together the night before. The last thing I remember was sitting at the bar ordering another drink while one by one my coworkers called it a night. I found out later that I had closed down the restaurant, and a coworker put me in an Uber to send me home. Never wanting the party to end, I jumped back out, bullied him into taking me to his apartment to meet his cats, ate all of his goldfish crackers, and passed out on his couch.

My phone was dead and my husband had no idea where I was.

Thankfully, Rick knew who was out with me that night and sent my coworker a message on Facebook. It wasn't long before he found me, drove the fifteen minutes to pick me up, and carried me home.

Like I said, it wasn't even the worst thing I had ever done. It wasn't the most shameful night, or the nastiest hangover. I was just tired. And so was Rick. I could see that he was slipping away, and the beautiful life we had built with him.

I had tried to quit before. I had made promises to moderate before. But this time, something was different. This time, I had finally had enough.

As I write this, I'm fifteen months sober. Not long in the grand scheme of things, but long enough to know I'm done.

I'm grateful to have had a privileged experience with quitting alcohol, and I want to say upfront that I know it doesn't feel this way for everyone. My privilege looked like this: a supportive husband who didn't drink much himself, financial stability that meant I had access to therapy and medication for the underlying depression and ADHD, and a body that didn't require medical detox. I had every advantage, and it was still one of the hardest things I've ever done in my entire life.

I don't identify as an alcoholic, and don't go to meetings. *Scandalous, I know.* What I do know is that I don't drink. *Ever.* I don't even consider it. One drink was never just one drink for me—it's twelve, eventually. Maybe not the first time, but addiction runs in my family, I have ADHD, and I carry a history of trauma. I know exactly where one drink leads, and I have no interest in going back.

I want to be clear: I'm not here to trash AA—it saves lives every day. But I knew that I needed a version of sobriety that fit me, my voice, and my history. What I know now is that healing is possible. I've had moments of clarity—moments where I've walked back into old rooms that once held nothing but pain and realized I no longer felt it the same way. Drowning those memories in poison and shame never freed me.

Sobriety did.

These rooms where I'm sober—the ones I'm building day by day—are different from all the others. Sobriety is now the foundation for every room I'm rebuilding. I carry it carefully, like an egg in my cupped hands. It's fragile. Some days, I can feel how thin the shell is, how easily it could crack. But it's also precious. It holds everything I've fought for: clarity, presence, the ability to show up for my family without shame clouding every moment.

Now, when I step into a room—literally or figuratively—I'm learning to walk in clear, awake, and unashamed. Some days are easier than others. But I'm here, and I'm sober, and that's everything.

The Room with
The Locked Door

I was diagnosed with ADHD the same week I decided to quit drinking. Ten days into sobriety, the diagnosis became official. I was forty-six years old. For those who know me, you're probably more surprised I didn't know sooner. But here we are.

It's a strange thing to be diagnosed halfway through your life with what you've always thought of as a little boy's condition. With age comes hindsight, though, and a whole lot of oh-shit-that-makes-sense-now moments. But before any clarity came a lot of grief.

I had to sit with the crushing weight of all the years I spent believing I was just broken.

I have always felt like a failure, like I was missing some essential adulting gene that everyone else got. Why couldn't I keep a house the way other women seemed to? I knew how to clean, so that wasn't it. When I finally caught up on housework, the place could sparkle. But the rest of the time? Cluttered. Dusty. A quiet hum of chaos in every corner.

I missed appointments and paid bills late. I forgot birthdays, and I spent decades convinced I was just lazy or careless. I called it "being scattered." I called it "being a mess." But it always made me feel like shit.

Once, I drove to three different stores looking for light bulbs, got distracted at each one, and came home with a yoga mat, a set of fancy dish towels, and a potted succulent. No light bulbs. I sat in the dark that night while I watered my new plant.

Now I know it was just my brain. I was wired differently and moving faster than the world around me, trying to survive in a system that demanded focus and consistency. What an awful thing to know—that I spent a lifetime punishing myself for something that was never a moral failing.

That ADHD diagnosis cracked open a door I didn't even know existed. Suddenly, so many of the rooms I've carried with me made more sense: the messy ones, the loud ones, the ones where I felt like I was too much.

Even in silence, my mind is like a crowded hallway: ideas, songs, half-finished conversations all bouncing off the walls. Every morning, I wake up with a song in my head. Not metaphorically. A literal song, full volume, first thing. Sometimes it's funny. More often, it's exhausting.

I used to think everyone lived like that. Now I just think: *no wonder I'm tired.*

After the diagnosis, I consumed everything I could about ADHD. The books, articles, podcasts, and YouTube videos. I learned that sleep is more important than Adderall. That feels rude, though, because I do love Adderall. The first time I took it, I almost cried. I sat at my kitchen table, staring at my coffee, and realized I could hear myself think. Just one thought. Then another. Not twelve at once.

Was this what everyone else's thoughts sounded like? Only one or two at a time?

The bizarre part about learning all this at forty-six is realizing I've carried it with me my entire life and didn't know it. It's like discovering a locked door inside your own house that's been there since childhood. You finally open it, and everything inside looks familiar, like it's been waiting for you.

That same week, I also stopped drinking. I realized the chaos in my head and the alcohol in my glass were in cahoots, conspiring to keep me from peace. Once I understood that my brain was working overtime just to exist, I realized the drinking wasn't helping me cope at all; it was adding static to an already overloaded system.

Ten days into sobriety, while raw, clear, and exhausted, I had already learned so much about both alcoholism and ADHD. I learned what alcohol was really doing for me—providing desperately-needed quiet, albeit temporarily—and what it was doing to me: creating anxiety, sleeplessness, shame, fatigue.

I learned about the strong link between ADHD and addiction. Understanding that connection gave me a new sense of compassion for myself. I wasn't weak. I was trying to self-soothe with the only thing that worked, even if just for a little while.

Here's what I know now: I'm not broken. I just need systems, structure, and space that fit the way my mind moves. I spent time re-organizing my house in a way that actually works for my brain. It's been over a year, and I've maintained those systems. I now set reminders for everything. I live and die by my calendar. I give myself grace when I still forget things, because that's part of the deal. And when I allow myself that, I can finally breathe.

The diagnosis didn't ruin me after all. It released me. It gave me language for the noise, and it let me stop apologizing for the way I'm wired and start honoring it instead.

ADHD isn't my downfall. It's my compass. It just took me forty-six years to find the map.

The Room Where I
Chose the Walls

It was May of 2023 and the woman standing beside my hospital bed was holding my hand, which should have been comforting. Instead, her words sent ice through my veins.

"Don't worry," she said. "I'm here from limb preservation."

Wait. What?

Limb preservation. That's a thing? That's a department with a title and person assigned to my case?

I looked down at my right foot, and it was gray. Ash-colored gray. The color of something that had already given up.

The arteries in both of my legs had closed and blood was no longer reaching my feet. I stared at them, willing them to look normal again, to flush pink with life.

But they didn't.

The panic that surged through me was sharp and familiar. It was the same dread I had carried into every hospital for years, the fear I'd promised myself I was learning to manage.

And here it was again. Only this time, it had teeth.

I had spent two years working on that fear—two years since my breakdown, trying to heal the wounds that had led me there. Part of that healing meant facing what hospitals had come to mean to me.

Our medical system does a decent job treating physical ailments, but the emotional toll of being sick, of being terrified, is largely ignored. I'd been admitted so many times: seven weeks on bedrest with Bella, meningitis that stole five days of my life, two cases of pneumonia, COVID, and more. Each time I walked through those sliding glass doors and smelled antiseptic, my body reacted before my brain could intervene.

Racing pulse. Tightening chest. The absolute certainty that the worst was happening again.

Because the worst had happened before.

I learned to recognize the fear when it came. I started meeting it with breath instead of panic. Slow inhale. Long exhale. A mantra whispered into the quiet: *You're here now. You're safe.* Sometimes I would journal straight from the hospital bed, pouring it all onto the page before it could take hold in my chest.

That's how I learned to steady myself. Not by pretending I wasn't afraid, but by staying present. Reminding myself that a headache is just a headache, that a twinge isn't impending doom.

It's not about erasing the fear. It's about proving to myself, again and again, that I can survive it.

But in 2023, lying in that bed with gray feet and a limb preservation specialist, I had to ask myself: *could I survive this?*

Nobody knew why this was happening to my legs and feet. The doctors were baffled. I was relatively young, a healthy weight, no diabetes, and arteries closed in both legs at the same time? They ran test after test, searching for answers. Meanwhile, the questions I had hung in the air, unspoken but obvious:

Would I walk out of this hospital? Would I lose a foot? Or both?

Here's what I expected to happen: I expected to spiral. To catastrophize. To let my mind run straight to worst-case scenarios and set up camp there, the way I always had before.

But I didn't.

When the fear came—and it came in waves—I breathed through it. When the "what ifs" started their familiar taunt, I pulled out my journal. I reminded myself as often as I needed to: just because your worst fears came true once doesn't mean they're coming true again. I wrote it out over and over.

During this hospital stay, I looked for, and found, joy in the small things: my daughter's daily visits, my husband's steady presence. The nurse who brought me a cup of coffee at three o'clock every afternoon, exactly the way I like it without me ever having to ask. The friend who threw me a full birthday picnic right there in the hospital room with sparkling cider in champagne glasses and the works, because I was spending my forty-fifth birthday in that room.

And somewhere between the machines beeping and the waiting and the coffee at three, something shifted. I found myself thinking: If I lose a foot, I will be okay. Even if I lose both feet, I will still be okay.

The thought didn't come with fanfare. It came quietly and settled into my chest like truth.

I will be okay.

Not because I wanted to lose my feet. Not because it wouldn't be devastating or life-changing. But because I finally understood what could not be taken from me: love, faith, and the people who show up to remind you that life is worth celebrating even when you're scared.

Joy isn't just about what we keep. It's about what remains when everything else is stripped away.

Now, when I sit with my patients who have been through their own personal nightmare, I hold their hands and help them breathe through the waves of anxiety and fear. And I tell them what I learned in that hospital room with my gray feet: just because the worst happened once doesn't mean it's happening again.

I can say it with the weight of experience behind it. Not as a platitude, but as the reality that I have lived.

Thankfully, my doctors restored the blood flow to my legs. They saved my feet. I walked out of that hospital on my own two legs, grateful beyond measure for the physicians' skill, their compassion, and their refusal to give up.

But what I carry with me most isn't the medical outcome. It's the choice I made while I was still in that room, the choice about how to decorate it while I was living in it.

That hospital room has become one of the brighter rooms I carry with me. When I walk back into it in my memory, I see love woven into the walls. I see joy shining through the cracks. I see the woman I was becoming, even as I was terrified of what I might lose.

Even though I was scared in the moment, I chose what to hang on those walls: gratitude, presence, connection, and hope.

And that choice? That's the one they can never take away.

The Room with Twelve Chairs

A friend called to ask if I had any folding chairs. She was hosting a lunch after her daughter's Christening—my goddaughter—and needed extra seating.

"I have twelve," I said.

Later, as I loaded the chairs into my almost brand-new Jeep, the metal cool against my palms, I could smell the vanilla buttercream from the two-tier cake I'd made sitting in the passenger seat. The chairs clanked against each other as I arranged them, trying to fit as many as I could.

And it hit me: I have an abundance.

The January before COVID, I made a vision board. It was arts and crafts for grown-ups: cut-out pictures and words glued to a canvas, meant to focus my intentions for the year ahead. Beaches. Organized spaces. Phrases like family time, adventure, abundance written out in fancy fonts.

Abundance was the word that stuck with me the most. At the time, I was hopeful for an abundance of money. But the universe had its own interpretation.

That year, I spent three months at home during lockdown recovering from COVID, and then another five when I broke my hip. I had an abundance of time with my family.

In the years that followed, abundance showed up in waves; some soft, some rough. There were incredible moments: a trip to Iceland, sobriety and the launch of my travel business. And there were devastating ones: losing my forty-three-year-old brother-in-law to cancer, facing my own darkness, surgeries, and hospital stays.

Abundance. You don't always see it while you're living it. But it's there; in what you have today compared to yesterday, in the rooms quietly filled with joy.

Growing up, everything we owned once belonged to someone else: the donated dresser, the hand-me-down couch, the toy box that smelled faintly of someone else's basement. For a while, our dining table was a wooden spool that once held telephone wire. The smaller one was our coffee table; rustic, but only because we were poor.

When we moved in with my stepdad, it was the opposite. We had furniture we weren't allowed to touch. A dining room with mauve chairs, a faux-stone table, and a bull skull centerpiece. Brian and I were not allowed to use that table. Instead, we ate at the kitchen island while my mother and stepdad ate in front of the television. Later, when my younger brother was old enough, he could eat in whatever room he wanted, including at that stone table.

Abundance has looked different at every stage of my life.

In my teens, it was extra time with friends: sleepovers where there was more laughing than sleeping, and talking until the sun came up.

In my twenties, it was enough money for my own apartment. I remember the day I bought my first real couch—not a hand-me-down, not something from the curb. Mine. I sat on it and cried.

In my thirties, it was Bella's laugh filling the house. Rick making coffee in the morning, the smell drifting across the house to wake me. Small, steady things that felt like safety.

In my forties, it's growth and healing. The ability to look back at the rooms I've carried and know I'm not trapped in them anymore.

What saddens me a little is realizing how often I missed it—the abundance that was already there. I was always reaching for more, measuring what was missing instead of what was overflowing.

Now, I'm learning to see abundance in all its forms. To feel it. To invite people in to share it.

Because sometimes abundance looks like twelve folding chairs. Enough for everyone to have a seat at the table.

The Room Where I
Took a Bath

One of the hardest parts of getting sober was figuring out who I was without alcohol. I carried this identity of being the "fun" girl for my entire adult life, whether that was true or not is up for debate.

But identity is a funny thing. It's so subjective.

At home, I'm a wife and mother, carrying the responsibility of making sure we never run out of toothpaste or clean underwear. I never feel like I'm winning that game, but I'm that April nonetheless.

At work, I'm a teacher. I facilitate independence, encourage recovery, and help patients see everything they're still capable of.

When I was drunk, I was fun. I was up for anything, always ready with a story, and collecting misadventures I could laugh about later. I performed a comedy set at a bar in Des Moines. I kneed a guy in the balls for grabbing my ass in a club. I laughed until I peed more times than I can even count. I thought I was a good time.

But identity swings both ways—the way you see yourself, and the way others see you.

While I seemed brave when I was five vodka clubs deep, I could also be obnoxious. Like the night I argued with a restaurant manager through our entire dinner because I thought someone had been seated out of order. Or the night I threw a remote at Rick in anger—while he was holding our infant daughter. That moment should have been my wake-up call. *It wasn't.*

The nights I fell and woke up bruised and bleeding. The days I threw up from morning to night. Any of those should have been a sign. But drinking had been a part of my life longer than anything else, so I held on.

Giving up alcohol meant saying goodbye to an identity I had carried my entire adult life. *Who the hell was I if I wasn't dancing on tables or making friends out of a bar full of strangers?* I didn't know the April who didn't carry the bravado of vodka.

At the time, I thought giving up alcohol meant I was going to lose a huge part of my life. Part of *me*. In a way, it felt like another amputation.

But sobriety didn't strip me down; it actually allowed me to rebuild. Without vodka, I got to meet the *real* April for the first time. And she turned out to be more than enough.

Meeting the real April also meant navigating what friendship looked like without alcohol at the center of it. Thankfully, Rick and I have the most beautiful group of friends.

Together, we are three couples with seven children between us. These incredible people are our chosen family. But raising kids takes time and energy, so our hangouts shifted from drunken game nights to carefully planned-out evenings, coupled with babysitters and shared calendars.

But for me, getting sober meant I wouldn't be the crazy one in our group anymore. So, I had to figure out who I was going to be.

Then came the "House of Yes" in Brooklyn.

We saw the ad for the Dirty Circus—Cirque du Soleil meets burlesque. We bought VIP tickets, because when we go out, we go all in. Our VIP booth had purple velvet seats and a table piled with tiny bottles of champagne and an all-you-can-drink menu. Thankfully, the House of Yes carries mocktails, so I ordered a nonalcoholic Paloma while everyone else popped their bubbly.

As the host of the circus—Pizza, a trans woman dressed as a slice—welcomed the crowd, she announced a raffle.

Man, I fucking love a raffle.

Nobody was required to buy a ticket, but if you bought one, the money supported The Trevor Project, a nonprofit providing crisis intervention and suicide prevention services to LGBTQ+ young people. The prize? Watching the rest of the show from a bubble-filled bathtub at the foot of the stage... if you stripped down to your underwear in front of the whole crowd first.

What. The. Actual. Fuck.

Okay, House of Yes—you got me. I bought so many raffle tickets I was basically guaranteed to win. And sure enough, twenty minutes later, Pizza pulled my number. My husband just laughed—because, of course I would do this. Luckily, the winner could bring a friend, and my partner-in-crime, Carleane, is just as nuts as I am.

So, hands shaking, mind racing, we walked onto the stage. *They weren't really serious about the stripping, right? That had to be a joke.*

And then, from stage right, the stage manager pantomimed peeling off his shirt. This was not a joke. This was happening.

The music kicked in, the lights dimmed, and a single spotlight hit us like a dare.

I was wearing a long black lace dress with buttons up the front. It was completely see-through. Underneath I wore a black halter top, a bra (*a cute one, thank God*), booty shorts, and my black combat boots. Oh—and a rubber spacer between my toes because: bunions.

I unbuttoned my dress and let it fall, trying to make tiny dance moves, with full awareness that I am not a dancer and definitely not a stripper. Next I pulled the halter top over my head, then reached down to remove my boots.

And then I froze: how the hell do you remove a toe spacer in a sexy way? Sexy and toe spacer don't even live in the same neighborhood. I quickly wrapped my hand around the end of my foot, slid the spacer out as discreetly as possible, and nervously tucked it into my boot laughing at the ridiculousness of this whole experience. Then I pulled off my bra.

They helped us into the tub, filled with lavender-scented bubble bath. The rest of the show was great. At intermission people came by our tub to congratulate us on our win. Rick and the rest of our group made their way over as well, and oddly enough he was so proud. I guess I didn't consider what his reaction would be to his wife stripping in front of at least a hundred strangers and then slipping into a bath. But there he was, grinning like an idiot, and I knew what he was thinking: She's still in there. The girl he fell in love with was still in there, just without the hangover the next morning.

When the show ended, we were handed towels and our clothes, but my booty shorts were soaked. A member of the staff handed us a bag of brand-new underwear. Play strange games, win strange prizes. I grabbed a pair of black Amazon Essentials bikini briefs, slipped them on under my see-through dress, and walked back out into the night.

We didn't go home after that. We had dinner down the street, then rooftop mocktails and cocktails at a bar a few blocks away. I spent the rest of the night in borrowed underwear, in a see-through dress, completely sober.

And I had more fun than I'd had in years.

Not because I was drunk. Not because I was numbing anything or performing for anyone. But because I was just... me. Ridiculous, awkward, bunion-spacer-removing me. And that was enough. When I look back, the House of Yes isn't just a memory, it's a new room I carry. A lighter room. The velvet, the lavender-scented bubbles, the spotlight—it's all there. And that room taught me that sobriety didn't mean I had to give up my misadventures. I just had to learn to walk into them as myself.

The Other Bathtub

Another bathtub, another ridiculous moment.

Sometimes I think I'm being cute and it works. Sometimes I embarrass myself in front of at least a hundred Christmas shoppers.

Settle in, kids, Grandma's got another story about the good ol' days.

Back when Amazon.com was just an online bookseller—seriously, we used to have to put on pants and leave the house to buy more pants—Christmas time was madness. We'd make a list of everyone we knew who deserved a gift, and we'd take that scrap of paper to an endless number of stores. Carrying bags. Waiting in lines. Walking. People.

It was a nightmare.

One year, I took on this mountain of a chore with my boyfriend at the time, Rick. We were at the mall, him carrying all the bags: a reading pillow from Sharper Image for his dad, an artsy metal décor plate for his uncle. We were shuffling through the crowds of all the other frantic Christmas shoppers when I spotted it.

You know how, in the center aisles of every mall, there are kiosks trying to sell you more stuff, without the inconvenience of having to walk into a store? Well, this mall had the company "Bath Fitter." Essentially, it was a bathtub with the shower stall built up around it on three sides, so you could picture your new tub/shower combo in all its glory.

Ever the weirdo, I decided it would be hilarious if I climbed into the tub and then called over to my boyfriend. He'd think I was so cute!

I ran ahead of him, practically giggling with excitement, and—headfirst, for reasons I still can't explain—tried to climb in.

In all my excitement over how funny this would be, I didn't see the plexiglass covering the entire display. The plexiglass that I just ran into, full steam, with my head.

Boi-oi-oi-oing!

You could hear the reverberation of my skull meeting that glass for, I don't know... miles, probably. The sound echoed through the whole wing of the mall. Shoppers stopped mid-stride. A kid pointed.

Rick watched the whole thing—me hunched over, hands on my head, half laughing, half crying—while what felt like a hundred Christmas shoppers stared at this grown-ass woman who thought she should climb into a bathtub at the mall.

This, of course, is the woman he married. Silly man.

The Room with
My Father's Ghost

The year I got married, 2009, I signed up for Ancestry.com to research my biological father. I thought maybe I could find him buried somewhere in the documents and family trees.

Instead, I found out he had died.

That's a strange realization. I couldn't really mourn a man I didn't know. Could I? But it still felt like a loss—like a door had shut on a room I never got a chance to enter. And now I never would.

It felt like he was right there, just on the other side of a door I couldn't open. As it turns out, you can find a lot more information about a person on Ancestry.com once they've passed. As his daughter, I was able to order his death certificate and see how he died, who listed him as next of kin, and what life he had built without me.

He had died of an accidental overdose.

I knew my father was an addict—it's one of the few things I'd been told from a young age. There was a story about him stealing someone's drugs at a party and then selling them back to the same person. The wild part? They actually bought them. If that story is true, I'm equal parts impressed and ashamed.

His next of kin was his wife, a woman in California. Her name was unique enough—and their town was small enough—that I found her social media account pretty quickly. She wasn't private, which felt like a strange kind of mercy.

I sat at my computer with the cursor hovering over her profile picture. My hands were shaking. I clicked.

I could see the outline of the life he had before he died.

The first thing I saw was their daughter. She was young, maybe four years old, and she looked so much like me at that age. It's unsettling to see your own face on a stranger. My heart broke for that little girl—my half-sister. Her father had died. Our father had died.

I scrolled deep into the woman's page, the way you might walk through a house quietly, touching the walls, trying to understand what happened there. I found posts about his sobriety, the injury that put him on pain medication, and the overdose that took his life in his sleep.

He had gotten better. He had built something. And then he was gone.

I closed the computer and cried—not for the man I lost, but for the story I never got to live. For the room that would forever stay locked.

Sixteen years later, in 2025, I got an email from a man who was a DNA match on my father's side, a second cousin. He'd been researching our shared family and wanted to share what he'd found.

I had spent years thinking that room had been locked forever. But here was someone handing me a key.

I opened it expecting a name or two, maybe a few dates of marriages and deaths. Instead, it was like he'd handed me the blueprint to an entire wing of my house I never knew existed.

He told me about Estella—my great-grandmother—who was born Anastasia in Lithuania in 1904. She came to America as a baby, renamed and reshaped by every new place she landed. She married four times, buried a child, and lived in Vienna after the war—in a palace with servants and soldiers.

My grandmother, Marylyn, grew up in that strange mix of privilege and pain before later moving back to America, where she married my grandfather, George Pope. They moved from New York to Kentucky when George joined the military, and there they had my father, Michael.

It was dizzying to learn all that history at once. Each name felt like a door clicking open somewhere in me. New rooms suddenly existed and were filled with movement.

Estella's story reminded me of my own in unexpected ways—the reinvention, the starting over, the surviving what should have broken her. She had crossed oceans and changed names to survive. She built a room for herself from nothing, brick by brick.

My grandmother had distanced herself from her mother, and my father from her. Generations of people who shut doors to protect themselves from the noise behind them.

And here I was, standing in the hallway of all of it—keys in hand.

When I read that Estella once listed her address as a "palace" in Vienna, I smiled. That word carried weight. Palace. For her, maybe it was marble floors and soldiers in uniforms. For me, it's the home I've built after the rubble. A home filled with laughter and extra chairs. A home where every locked room is slowly being aired out, one by one.

When I look back now, I can see the pattern so clearly—every generation trying to build something more stable than the one before, but each of us working with damaged materials. We're all building palaces from rubble.

Estella built from survival. She crossed oceans and started over again and again, patching her foundation with grit and grief.

My grandmother, Marylyn, built from anger and distance. Her walls were sturdy but cold. She locked the door on her mother's room and never looked back.

My father tried to build from hope. His walls were uneven—bright in some places, crumbling in others—and eventually, they gave way.

And then there's me.

For a long time, I thought I was building something new. But really, I was rebuilding the same house from old blueprints; fear, perfectionism, and self-protection disguised as independence.

It wasn't until everything fell apart—my health, my drinking, the night I couldn't do it anymore—that I realized the house I was trying to live in wasn't safe.

I needed to rebuild. But this time from joy.

When I became a mother, I started seeing every choice through a different lens. I didn't want Bella to inherit these locked doors. I wanted her to know that she could walk freely through all the rooms—hers and mine—even the ones that hurt. That she could sit in her sadness, name it, and still believe in light.

Some days, I feel the weight of my family before me; Estella's strength, Marylyn's silence, my father's struggle. They're all here, somewhere in these walls. But now, instead of trying to seal them off, I'm learning to honor them; to walk into their rooms and say, "Thank you. I'll take it from here."

And when I think about the generations still to come—Bella, her children, maybe theirs—I hope they never have to search for their family through death records or ancestry databases. I hope they'll find their roots right here, in the laughter that echoes through these walls, in the extra chairs, in the rooms that stay unlocked.

So, I finally found my father. Not in a database. I found him in the quiet understanding that every generation does the best they can with the materials they have—and that it's my turn now to rebuild differently.

This time, the foundation is gratitude. The framework is love. The walls are lined with joy.

And the door? It's open.

The Rooms We No
Longer Share

B rian lives in Texas now and I'm in New York. We only speak every few years.

The last room we shared was the one where I got married here in New York, almost seventeen years ago.

It's been decades since the moment in the police station. I didn't ruin my family that day, but it is the day everything changed between Brian and me forever. We were never the same after that.

There's no real animosity between us now. We're just very different people. He's a talented craftsman, building kitchens and decks for people who commission his work, and I admire his talent from afar.

My baby brother Chris lives in Hawaii. He is a missionary, traveling the world and sharing his faith. I'm so proud of him and thankful that he comes to visit his big sister in New York every few years.

For a short time, Chris moved into a room in my house in New York and lived with us. I had left California when he was five years old and missed most of his childhood. For these wonderful six months, we got to know each other again.

There was a time I was scared I would lose him to depression and anxiety; they were breaking him. Living with us gave him space to heal, and I'm so proud of who he's become.

The last time I saw Chris was a few years ago, when his father died. I had no love left for his father and wouldn't have attended the funeral if Chris didn't need me. But I flew across the country, without my family, to help my baby brother grieve the man who never stepped in to protect us, the man who spent too many nights making things worse, making our lives more unstable. I went to make sure Chris wasn't pulled back into depression, or overrun by anxiety, and to help make that room—the one where he celebrated his father's life—worthy of the love they had for each other. Thank God I was there, because my brother didn't even realize he needed to order food for his guests.

I wasn't sober yet. The night I departed from California, I sat in the airport bar and drank. I drank for every feeling I felt in California. That state holds my childhood, every room of it. Even then, with Chris having grown up, my stepdad gone, and me having a family of my own three thousand miles away, I still couldn't let myself feel the full weight of what that place, and the people in it, made me feel.

It's funny, really. I boarded the flight to California feeling like the responsible big sister, but I returned home realizing how much of the little girl I still was.

And my mother... well, my mother is still my mother.

The rooms my mother lives in are sometimes painful, sometimes filled with shame, and occasionally even silly. There are layered, complicated emotions stored in all of those memories. Almost every room I carry from before my healing journey has a dark corner where I keep the weight of her energy.

When I open those doors to the rooms my mother lives in, I try to think about how she must have felt in those moments. Was it the distance she felt from her own mother that kept her from getting too close to me? Was it the abuse from her father that led to those dark bursts of violence? Was it a lifetime of struggle that blinded her to the joy she could have felt in knowing her only grandchild?

My story is her story; she placed the furniture in so many of my rooms. There are pieces of her in me. I hear her voice sometimes when I speak. I see her feet when I look down at mine, her cheekbones when I catch my reflection. It's hard to be bound so deeply to the person who was supposed to keep me safe, but instead, taught me how to feel unsafe.

She did try, though. Shining a light on only her failures would be unfair. My mother was raising two small children on her own while attending college to become a respiratory therapist. She worked as much as she could to make sure we had a place to live, food on the table, and a few gifts at Christmas. During the times she couldn't sustain the momentum, she would break and send us away.

But she always came back.

I tend to assign a sinister motive to her return, as if the only reason she took us home was because someone else was raising us better than she could. But that, too, is unfair. She wouldn't have come back at all if she didn't truly miss and love her children. There was always an undertone of love, even if it should have been the overtone.

I wish I had more lighthearted memories with my mother. It's not that they don't exist. I remember her dancing in the kitchen once, singing along to Whitney Houston. I remember her laughing at something I said, her whole face lighting up. Those moments are locked away in rooms I can't reach yet—glimpses, but no full scenes. Fragments of moments, but nothing to hold on to. I pray that as I open more doors and bring light into more rooms, I'll get them back and find the ones I've been missing.

I believe I'll always be working through my memories and my relationships with my brothers and our mother. I'll always wrestle with the feeling that Chris was treated better, that Brian turned on me in that police station, that my mother carries more pride for them and more judgment for me.

But this is where we are now: scattered across the country, living separate lives, connected by blood and history, not by closeness. We aren't estranged, but we are not family in the way I once thought family should be.

And maybe that's okay. Maybe this is what healing looks like—not reconciliation, not rupture, but distance with understanding. They are who they are. I am who I am. The rooms we shared still exist, but I don't have to live in them anymore.

I have built new rooms. Rooms filled with the family I've chosen, the friends who became like sisters, the husband who stays, the daughter who will never wonder if she was loved enough. Those rooms are bright and warm and safe. And sometimes, when I'm ready, I walk back into the old ones. Not to live there, but to remember. To honor what was. To forgive what wasn't. And then I close the door gently behind me and walk back into the light.

The Room I Was
Meant to Build

I was seventeen years old, driving a 1981 Ford Mustang that smelled like rotten cooked eggs, somewhere on the 405 in bumper-to-bumper traffic, holding a printout with an address in Los Angeles.

This was 1995. No GPS. No MapQuest. Just me and a Thomas Guide—a book of maps that lived under the driver's seat of every car back then. I had looked up the street in the back of the guide, found the coordinates, and traced my route across pages and pages of unfamiliar freeways with my finger. A ballroom in a big hotel. An audition for the American Musical and Dramatic Academy in New York City.

The audacity of it still gets me.

That car was one of a kind. The horn was on the turn signal, so sometimes I would accidentally honk at other drivers when trying to merge. The radiator was damaged, and a friend told me I could fix it by pouring raw eggs into it. Raw eggs in the radiator. Why? I don't know. But I did it, because we didn't have the internet, okay? Radiators get hot—that's why fluid pumps through them. Those eggs cooked on the first drive, and that car smelled like rotten cooked eggs for the rest of its short life.

I came from small beginnings. A small family. Small dreams. Just survival. That was the scale my life was measured on. Get through, get by, don't expect too much.

But that day, driving to L.A. in a car held together by junkyard parts and misguided advice, I wanted more.

After a couple of hours in Southern California traffic, I arrived at my audition— a large ballroom with parquet floors, my voice echoing back at me in a room that suddenly felt much bigger than I was. That day was my first taste of something bigger. I could see the bright lights, feel the pulse of the city. For just a moment, I believed in the possibility that maybe I had a place on a stage instead of in the shadows.

But fear has a funny way of getting loud when your dreams get big.

When the acceptance came, with a scholarship, I held my future in my hands.

I stood in my mother's kitchen, that envelope in my hand, and I could feel the weight of it. New York. A stage. A life that was mine.

And then, terrified, I threw it away.

The voice in me that told me I didn't belong sounded a lot like my mother's. The girl who wasn't worth a Girl Scout vest certainly wasn't worth Broadway dreams. Who was I to think I belonged in New York, on a stage, in a world full of people braver and more talented than I was?

So, I let it win. I told myself I couldn't, that a life that big was meant for other people. I stayed small. I stayed safe. I chose survival over possibility, the way I'd been taught.

Looking back now, I see how often I tried to keep my life small. But the universe never stopped tugging at me.

Meningitis showed me that I could beat the odds. Occupational therapy school—which I finally attended at thirty-five—reminded me that I could do anything if I just focused my energy. And eventually, sobriety, healing, and the courage to tell my own story kept pulling me forward.

The irony still makes me laugh: I thought I had walked away from New York, afraid to be who I was meant to be. But here I sit, in my house on Long Island, raising my family years later, just a short train ride from the city I once ran away from.

Only now, instead of telling stories in other people's voices, I'm telling my own—writing it down, speaking it out loud, refusing to let it stay hidden in the shadows where I once kept myself.

The girl who threw away her acceptance letter would never believe that one day, she'd have the courage to stand in her own story.

But here I am.

The Meeting

I love Jason Mraz. I've been listening to his music since before The Remedy, his first big hit, was even on the radio. I was in my early twenties when I first heard his lyrical genius, and I was obsessed. He's been with me ever since—twenty-five years of songs that have been the soundtrack to every stage of my life. His music speaks to me.

So, when there was an opportunity to meet him in New York City, I was going to be there—even if I had to be carried. I had just gotten out of the hospital and could only walk short distances, so my friend (also a huge fan) drove us into Manhattan and pushed me through the city in a wheelchair.

The line to meet him wrapped around the Barnes & Noble on Fifth Avenue. We were disappointed by how long it was, but we were not defeated.

As we reached the end of the line, a man wearing an official vest approached and asked us to follow him. That beautiful soul walked us—well, they walked, my friend pushed me—past the line of fans who'd been waiting for hours. He led us right to the front.

Suddenly, Jason Mraz was sitting twenty feet away.

We had spent the drive into the city belting out our favorite songs, reminiscing about concerts, the time we saw him on Broadway, and how each album had spoken to a different season of my life. Every song felt like comfort food.

And that's what I decided I would tell him—that his music was comfort food.

I practiced it in my head as we got closer. Comfort food. Simple. Honest. Perfect.

When the moment came and my friend wheeled me up to him, Jason stood and gave me a hug. I opened my mouth, heart pounding, ready to share what his music meant to me.

"Hi," I said. "I'm such a big fan. I like food."

Shit.

My friend's hand flew to her mouth and she laughed out loud. Jason smiled kindly as I sat there in my wheelchair, mortified, replaying what had just come out of my mouth.

I like food.

Not "your music is comfort food for my soul." Not "your songs have carried me through so much." Just... I like food.

He was gracious. He signed my album, took a photo, and hugged me again. But as my friend wheeled me away, I could feel my face burning.

"Did I really just say that?" I asked.

"You really did," she said, trying not to laugh.

Twenty-five years of fandom, three hours in traffic, and all I managed to tell Jason Mraz was that I like food.

But you know what? At least it was true.

The Rooms Where
I Found Peace

Bella was having a yard sale to raise money for a local cat café. We had adopted a fourteen-year-old cat named Piper and loved him for four months before he passed. Bella, just eleven years old, wanted to make sure that "every senior cat gets a loving home." She wanted to help pay for adoption fees and medical care to remove the barriers to these cats being adopted.

We planned a yard sale, and people from all over our community donated items we could sell. The day of the sale, the money poured in. One man bought a small lamp with a price tag of two dollars and paid with a fifty-dollar bill. "No change," he said, donating the rest to the cause. The entire day was exhausting, but a beautiful testament to the goodness of people.

Bella raised $1,400 that day.

Later that weekend, I called my mother to tell her all about Bella's yard sale and how proud I was of her. I also know that my mother is an animal lover and thought she might want to contribute a little something to her granddaughter's cause.

"We raised fourteen hundred dollars," I told her, trying to keep the pride out of my voice but failing.

"That's nice," she said. I could hear a slight smile in her voice, but also the distraction that always accompanied her calls. She was already thinking about something else.

"Bella worked so hard," I continued. "People came from all over. One man paid fifty dollars for a two-dollar lamp and told us to keep the change."

"Mm-hmm. That's cool."

I gripped the edge of the kitchen counter, hoping she was soaking in what I was saying. "We're still accepting donations if you want to contribute before we announce the final total."

Silence.

"No," she replied.

Not "I wish I could." Not "Tell Bella I'm proud of her." Not even "That's wonderful."

Just *no*.

My chest tightened. That familiar ache spread through my ribs—the certainty that I wasn't worth her effort, her pride, her ten dollars.

"Okay," I said quietly. "I'll let you go."

I hung up and stood there, staring at the sink, my phone still warm in my hand. The kitchen felt smaller suddenly, the air heavier. It was like all the rooms that carried the disappointment I felt from her, I was in all of those rooms all at once. I tried so hard not to get angry, but I felt my face flush and that familiar sickness in my stomach. "What the fuck?" I thought as tears filled my eyes.

I wrote about this exchange in my journal the next morning, and I was pissed. How could she not even send ten dollars? Or forget the money—just tell me you're proud. Proud of Bella for working so hard. Proud of me for raising a girl who sees a need in the community and tries to help. Anything besides "No."

But as I wrote, my tone changed and my heart began to settle.

I had decided weeks before this event that I was going to be more forgiving—about the past, about the abuse and neglect. I knew I needed to change and pick the path of peace, knowing that I couldn't change anything that had happened. I could only move forward carrying that burden, or choose freedom from it.

I had decided to change. She hadn't.

I found, while writing in my journal, that I was judging her behavior based on the idea that she had promised to be different.

But she hadn't. I did.

I promised myself that I would let her journey be hers, and my journey mine. That I wouldn't let her shortcomings trigger me and pull me back into those rooms from when I was a kid.

And it was in that moment, writing in that journal, that I could breathe easier and see the path ahead. It was lighter, brighter, and so much less angry.

The work of that promise started small. With breath. With awareness. With practice.

But journaling alone wasn't always enough. Some mornings, I couldn't even pick up the pen without grounding myself first. The anger, or anxiety, was too loud; my thoughts were spinning too fast. That's when I'd use the 5-4-3-2-1 technique my therapist taught me: five things I could see, four things I could touch, three things I could hear, two things I could smell, and one thing I could taste. It pulled me out of my head and back into my body anchoring me in the present moment.

Starting therapy was hard for me. I don't like not being good at things, and I definitely don't like asking for help. So, therapy feels as if I'm admitting I'm not good at anything, and I need a lot of help. Yuck. But it's also one of the most important things I've ever done.

My first therapist wasn't equipped to handle me—and I wasn't ready to do the work. I manipulated the sessions to avoid talking about anything real, and she couldn't break through my walls.

My next therapist was better. He was a retired New York City Police Officer who counseled trauma survivors and first responders from September 11, 2001. He was also a recovering alcoholic, which mattered in my early sobriety. He taught me grounding techniques that I still use today.

In one session, I finally said out loud that my mother's abuse wasn't my fault. That I was just a child. That I should have been loved and protected. Hearing those words come out of my own mouth changed something deep inside me. For the first time, I could separate what happened to me from who I am.

Therapy wasn't a magic fix. Some sessions I left feeling lighter. Others left me feeling worse, like every box from the attic had been dumped on the floor. But then, in the quiet moments, something would shift. A phrase would echo for weeks, or I'd respond differently to something that used to trigger me. That's the real work: not fireworks, but small flickers of progress.

When I first heard about Reiki, I was skeptical. Someone waving their hands over me without touching me—how was that going to help?

But it did.

I lay on a massage table under a blanket, spa music playing softly, the smell of incense burning. I had a lightly weighted eye mask covering my eyes that smelled of lavender. Within a few minutes of closing my eyes, my body softened like I'd been holding my breath for years and finally let it out.

Reiki feels like someone taking the heaviness in my soul and replacing it with air. The static in my head was finally quiet. The buzzing in my chest eased.

Reiki taught me that not all healing has to come from words. I love therapy and journaling, but I can only talk about my wounds so much. Eventually, I need something that helps clear chaotic energy from my body. Reiki does that for me.

The practice moved me so deeply that eventually I became a Reiki practitioner myself. Now I get to create quiet rooms where others can let go of what they've been carrying.

I used to think healing meant storming into every locked room and ripping the boards off the windows. Reiki showed me that some rooms don't need force; they need gentleness. Sometimes the most powerful healing comes in whispers, not shouts.

Processing pain through journaling and therapy was essential. Releasing it through Reiki helped. But none of that was enough if I wasn't also building joy. I needed to fill my life with things that reminded me I was more than my trauma.

So I started saying yes.

Starting in 2020, when the world shut down, I tried everything: sewing, crocheting, laser engraving, painting Dungeons & Dragons miniatures with Rick. Some things stuck, some didn't. But the act of trying became its own kind of healing. I was creating pockets of time where joy was allowed to live.

Saying yes to small joys built the foundation for bigger ones. But here's what I learned: tools are only as strong as the hands that hold them. And sometimes, my hands weren't strong enough.

Journaling helped me process. Therapy gave me insight. Reiki released what I couldn't name. Joy reminded me I was alive.

But when the rooms got too dark, when the weight was too heavy, when my own strength ran out—I needed something more. Something bigger than myself to lean on.

I needed a source.

Service became that source.

Growing up the way I did, and with all the trouble I caused for myself in my twenties, I needed a lot of help. People stepped in when I had nothing to offer, when I didn't even know what to ask for. Teachers who saw potential I couldn't see. Neighbors who fed me when my mother wouldn't. Friends who let me sleep on their couches when home wasn't safe.

For years, I carried shame about that. About being the one who always needed saving.

I'm a doer. I make magic shows out of thin air, I sign up for sports I've never tried, and I work in occupational therapy. I fix things. I help. It's in my bones. But for the longest time, I was only doing for myself—building my life, protecting my family, creating distance from the past.

Then I started serving others. I began fundraising for a family in crisis, planning events that raised thousands of dollars. I established the JD BUILDS Foundation to support youth pursuing careers in the trades—kids who might need someone to believe in them the way people once believed in me. I stepped up to help when people needed it.

And something unexpected happened.

The first time I helped organize a fundraiser, I watched a hundred people show up for someone they barely knew. I saw strangers write checks, donate items, volunteer their time. The room was thick with love—real, tangible love. And I realized: this is what people did for me when I was young. This is what it looked like from the other side.

Every event I planned, every dollar raised, every person touched—it wasn't just helping someone else. It was healing that young girl who once felt like a burden. Who thought she only took and never gave. Who believed she didn't deserve the help she received.

Service showed me I had become the person I needed when I was young. It's not just true that it's better to give than receive. It's transformative.

When you've spent your life feeling helpless—watching bad things happen and not being able to stop them—there's something profoundly healing about finally having the power to help. To show up. To be the person who doesn't look away.

Service gave me something I would never have: the ability to make a difference. Not just in my own life, but in someone else's. And in learning to give without expecting anything in return, I found I was no longer that scared kid with empty hands. I had become someone who could create change, ease burdens, offer hope.

Service became my room—a place where pain transformed into purpose, where shame became strength, where all that heaviness I'd been carrying finally had somewhere useful to go.

The Room Where
God Was Different

People have told me more times than I can count that I'm brave. Brave for surviving meningitis. Brave for living with kidney disease. Brave for raising my daughter, for getting sober, for sharing my story.

First of all? That's hilarious. Brave? Me? I don't feel brave. I feel like I'm just putting one foot in front of the other, and some days I'm barely holding myself together.

But here's what I've learned: bravery isn't about feeling brave. It's about not feeling brave—and showing up anyway.

Bravery is standing in the doorway of the rooms you've been too afraid to open and saying, "Okay, let's do this." It's making the therapy appointment. It's choosing joy in the middle of grief. Not because the pain isn't real, but because it isn't everything.

And when I've needed that kind of courage—the kind that carries you when you can't carry yourself—I've found it in my faith.

Now, before you skip this chapter because faith isn't your thing, hear me out. Your source of strength doesn't have to look like mine. Maybe yours is nature; standing barefoot in the grass, feeling connected to something ancient. Maybe it's community; friends who show up when you can't ask for help. Maybe it's art, music, science, or the quiet certainty that the sun will rise tomorrow no matter how dark tonight feels.

What I learned is this: we all need something to lean on when our own strength runs out.

For me, that's God. But I almost lost that connection because of how my mother used it.

My mom is a born-again Christian. She wielded scripture like a hammer and forgiveness like a hall pass. I have a vivid memory of her telling me once that the devil was working through me because I took too long a shower, which meant my stepdad wouldn't have enough time to get ready for church. I was fourteen years old. Water and soap became a weapon. Her faith wasn't about love. It was about control.

She used God as her shield. "Yes, I'm a sinner, but God forgives me." The unspoken implication was always: "If God does, then you should too." That was her pattern: sin, apology, forgiveness, repeat. It left me wondering if she even wanted to change, or if she just used God's mercy as an excuse not to.

Growing up with that twisted version of God left me choking on the word itself. The God she preached was not the one I wanted.

But here's the miracle: even in that mess, something bigger than me still found me. Not in stuffy pews or lengthy sermons, but in the quiet moments where I should not have survived but did. In the ICU when machines were breathing for me. When my body failed again and again, and yet somehow, I got another chance.

The God I know now doesn't care if I take a long shower. He can work around it. He cares if I show up, if I love people, and if I keep trying, even when it's hard. He doesn't hover with a clipboard, tallying sins. He's with me in my pain and heartbreak, in my joy and my efforts.

Here's how my God is different from hers:

Her God demanded perfection. Mine accepts me in progress.

My mother's faith required performance; the right clothes for church, the right words in prayer, the right appearance of holiness. Any mistake was evidence of the devil working through you. My faith? It meets me in my yoga pants on the bathroom floor. It doesn't require me to have it all figured out before I show up.

Her God was found in pews. Mine met me in the ICU.

She found God in Sunday services and scripture study groups. I found Him when machines were breathing for me, when my body was failing, when I had nothing left to offer but the fact that I was still here. He didn't wait for me to clean up before He showed up. He was already there, in the beeping monitors and the hands of nurses and the impossible fact that I survived.

Her God kept score. Mine keeps company.

My mother wielded God like a weapon; every sin tallied, every mistake proof you weren't faithful enough. The God I know sits with me in my worst moments. When I was drinking myself to death, He didn't abandon me. When I was making the same mistakes over and over, He didn't give up. He waited. Not with judgment, but with an open door for whenever I was ready.

Her God required forgiveness without change. Mine asks for both.

My mother's pattern was sin, apologize, receive forgiveness, repeat, with no actual transformation. She used God's mercy as permission to keep hurting people. My faith asks something harder: it asks me to actually change. To do the work. To show up in therapy, to stay sober, to break the cycles. Forgiveness isn't a hall pass to keep doing harm—it's fuel to become better.

Her God spoke through fear. Mine speaks through love.

I grew up believing God was watching, waiting for me to mess up so He could punish me. The God I know now? He's not waiting for me to fail. He's cheering for me to succeed. He doesn't use my trauma against me, He walks with me through it. When I'm afraid, He doesn't tell me the devil is working through me. He reminds me I'm stronger than I think.

This is why I almost walked away from faith entirely. Because her version of God was suffocating, controlling, and impossible to please. But when I let go of her God and found my own? Everything changed.

I don't go to church every Sunday. I don't quote scripture to prove I'm faithful enough. I don't perform my faith for anyone's approval.

Instead, I pray in my car on the way to work. I find God in the sunrise over the bay, in my daughter's laugh, in the quiet certainty that I'm not doing this alone. I practice my faith by showing up; for my family, for my healing, for the hard work of becoming someone I'm proud to be.

Faith became a room in my castle that I struggled to claim publicly. A sacred space where the weight wasn't so heavy, where I wasn't defined by what had happened to me. For a long time, I was too afraid to open that door because I thought it would still hold my mom's voice. But when I finally did, I found something else entirely: love, mercy, and light.

Faith doesn't solve everything. It didn't undo what happened to me. But it gives me the courage to keep going. To step into the hard rooms, to do the painful work, and to believe that I am worth more than my worst moments. That's where bravery and my source of strength intersect: faith gives me the strength to be brave, and bravery allows me to live my faith authentically instead of performing someone else's version of it.

But maybe for you, it's not faith. Maybe it's the unconditional love of your dog, the way the ocean reminds you that you're part of something vast, your grandmother's voice saying "You can do hard things," or music that moves through your body and reminds you you're alive.

The question isn't if you're brave enough. The question is: what will you lean on when you need to be?

Because if you've survived the things that tried to break you—and you have, because you're here reading this—you've already found something to lean on, even if you haven't named it yet.

And if your idea of God, or love, or safety has been twisted by people who used those words for harm, know this: they don't get the final word. They don't own it. You can build your own room of strength, where whatever you believe in meets you as you are, not as anyone else told you to be.

Bravery isn't about never falling apart. It's about knowing where to find your strength when you do.

The Room Where
Joy Lives

As I found my way out of my grief and darkness, I felt drawn to a particular feeling: joy. And from that, I started something that I call The Find Your Joy Project. For about a year, I held events for my friends and family, women who were looking for something more than the day to day and the taking care of everything for everyone else. We learned crafts like crochet and macrame. We challenged ourselves with a pole dancing exercise class and learned makeup techniques from a professional. We got creative in the kitchen with royal icing cookies and paella. We tried new things and some things brought us joy, and some didn't. But there was joy in the trying.

Before joy, there was a numbness so complete I couldn't name it. The days blurred together. Getting out of bed felt like a monumental task, and I moved through hours like I was wearing weights. I wasn't living; I was surviving. And I knew, somewhere deep down, that surviving wasn't enough.

That's when the word found me: joy.

It's funny how I never even noticed the word joy before then. But once it did, I started seeing it everywhere: on T-shirts, coffee mugs, Instagram quotes, church signs.

Was it always there? Probably. Still, I couldn't help asking myself: What the hell does it even mean?

It's not happiness. It's something different. Something deeper.

I've learned you can't have joy without sadness. It's the contrast that makes joy recognizable. But I would take it even further: it's the growth that comes from grief, trauma, stress, loss, and sadness. That's where joy is born. I kept asking myself: how?

Finding joy on the good days is easy. The days when you wake up to birds singing, your family surprises you with breakfast, your outfit has pockets, your hair is perfect, and everyone thinks you're amazing. That is joy on a platter.

But what about the other days? The days when life hands you rotten lemons and then squirts one in your eye. The days of shocking losses, gut-punch news, and moments that change you forever.

What does joy have to do with those days?

Here's what I know: there is a time and place for gratitude, but when you're in crisis, that's not it. Telling someone to "just be grateful" when their life is falling apart is dismissive. You know those people who say, "It could be worse"? Yeah, but it could also be a hell of a lot better.

My advice on those days is simple: grieve. Don't avoid it. Don't gloss it over with platitudes. You cannot heal a pain you won't acknowledge. You cannot heal if you don't first feel.

But after you've honored the grief, you have to come back to life. Grieve, but don't set up permanent residence in grief's abyss. Visit, but don't live there. Take your moment and then come back. Like at the end of meditation: wiggle your fingers and toes, nod your head, breathe deep, and when you're ready, open your eyes.

Because believe it or not, joy persists.

It lives just outside the abyss, and it looks different there. It's not beach vacations, champagne toasts, or belly laughs. In grief, joy comes in like tiny grains of sand: clean pajamas, a hot shower, the first breath that doesn't catch in your throat.

I know this because I have traveled there: depression, illness, COVID, a broken hip, emergency room visits, and a night I almost didn't make it. And still, here I am.

The real joy isn't the big stuff. It's the breath itself. A grain of sand. A starting point.

Joy changes everything.

First, it makes it easier to deal with other people, and you know how people can be. I like to think of joy as Tylenol for the soul. It brings your emotional pain scale down.

You've heard doctors ask, "On a scale from one to ten, with ten being the worst pain imaginable, how bad is your pain?" What if we applied the same scale to our emotions? On any given day, at any time, you can stop and check your number. Right now, I'm at a six. But when I'm running at an eight or nine, it doesn't take much for me to hit a ten, and I explode.

That's why seemingly small annoyances push us over the edge. If you're already at a nine, it only takes a tiny poke to unleash the bear.

Let me paint you a picture:

It's been a year. You've had loss, illness, and financial hardship. Your sandwich bread is moldy, you're out of ham, your husband ate your leftovers, and the dog just puked on the rug. You are currently at a nine.

Now your sweet little Jimmy comes home from school, full of stories about races, friends, and a teacher who sneezed so hard she had to leave the room. You're trying to stay present until he casually says, "Oh, by the way, I lost my lunch box."

And you explode.

Now, the sliding-doors version: You've had loss, but you journaled about it and shared with friends, so you're not carrying it alone. You've been sick, but you gave your body rest because the floors can wait. You've faced financial hardship, but you've found free ways to have fun. The dog pukes; you wash the rug and move on. You took fifteen minutes this morning to journal, meditate, sing, draw, or call a friend. You're at a six.

Jimmy comes home, tells the same story; races, jumping, sneezing, and the lost lunch box. But this time, you have the space to take a breath. You send him with another bag tomorrow, plan to buy a new one on the weekend. He helps with the dishes to earn it. No explosion.

Joy didn't erase the problems. It gave you the buffer to respond with grace.

I want to tell you about my Great Aunt Jean. Looking back, I feel bad calling her this, but as a kid, I thought she was a bitch. She was one of those I'm just being honest people, but never when it was something kind. Her face was in a chronic scowl. I don't know that I ever saw her smile.

Uncle Sandy, her husband, was the total opposite. He was jolly and silly, the kind of man who could fill any room with laughter. He had a big, hard belly like Santa Claus, and his face hardly had a wrinkle. He was always smiling.

When Uncle Sandy died, Aunt Jean didn't change. If anything, she complained more.

Then one day, over lunch with a friend, she confessed that as a little girl, she'd always wanted to take tap-dancing lessons, but her parents wouldn't let her. She had carried that grudge for seventy years.

Her friend finally snapped and said, "Jean, if you want to take a tap class, then take a tap class. You're an adult. Quit your bitching and sign up already."

And so, at seventy-six years old, Aunt Jean did exactly that. She enrolled in a tap class at her local senior center, and she loved it. She got to be silly. She got proud. And for the first time, I saw her smile like she meant it. She even performed in a recital.

Aunt Jean softened. Joy had cracked open her hardness and let some light in.

It breaks my heart that Uncle Sandy wasn't alive to see his wife finally discover joy. But Aunt Jean's story is a reminder not to wait until you're seventy-six to take the leap. Try the thing you've always wanted to try. Be a little silly. Be a little brave.

I didn't expect to find my own answer in a movie theatre, of all places. But sometimes the universe speaks up when you're finally ready to listen.

Reclining seats. Too many snacks. My daughter and I dressed in pink, ready for a silly night watching the Barbie movie. But instead of being silly, I cried like a schoolgirl.

There was one line that lodged itself in me. Rhea Perlman says, "We mothers stand still so our daughters can look back to see how far they've come."

At first, I thought it was beautiful. But the more I sat with it, the more I hated it.

I don't want to stand still. I don't want my daughter to look back and see me frozen in place, waiting for her to outgrow me. I want her to see me moving, learning, creating, and adventuring. I want her to see that being a mother isn't the end of your story. It's part of a much bigger, vibrant life.

Joy isn't passive. It isn't standing still. It's choosing to keep moving. This brings me to one of my favorite rooms of all: the craft room.

It started in January 2020, just before the pandemic, when Rick bought me a sewing machine. We'd been walking through a craft store, and I casually mentioned, "One day I want to learn to sew." He picked up a sewing machine and put it in the cart. That's the kind of man he is.

At first, I set up on the dining table, making crooked pillows and lopsided projects, but soon Rick emptied the guest room and built me a sewing desk. A few months later, when the pandemic hit and the world held its breath, I would close the door to that room and sew. I made terrible masks, random practice pieces, and a pile of projects that never quite worked. But in that room, I could breathe. The pandemic wasn't allowed in there. Chaos wasn't allowed in there.

Later, I tried other things like Cricut crafts and crocheting. Some things I loved, some not so much. But every time I sat at that table in my bright, airy room, the energy shifted. The weight lifted.

I found my joy again, in that room. That room is safe and holds no heartbreak or shame. I was never a mess in that room. I was inspired and brave enough to try new things.

I made joy in that room.

Joy isn't waiting for me at the finish line. It's what carries me through the hardest miles. It can be small, imperfect, fleeting, but powerful enough to keep me here, moving forward, one breath at a time.

The Room I Will
Keep Building

I used to think healing meant closing doors. Now I know it means opening them, even the ones I'd rather keep sealed. Every time I walk through another room, I find a new piece of myself waiting inside. And maybe, when I finally step back far enough, I'll see that all these rooms, even the dark ones, were part of something bigger I was building all along.

My life started small. Small family, small dreams, living moment to moment, just surviving. But I don't live small anymore. I've built a big life, one filled with big love, big hope, and big joy.

And now, I want you to know something: you deserve a big life too.

The castle you live in—the one made of your memories, your choices, your hurts, your hopes—is yours to build and rebuild as many times as you need. You don't have to stay in rooms that suffocate you. You don't have to settle for spaces that keep you small. You have permission to redecorate, to open the windows, to let in light.

I am forty-seven years old, and I am not done healing. Some rooms in my castle still hold fear, shame, and grief. I know it will take more time, more energy, more tools to work through everything I've carried. But here's the truth: the thing that's helped me heal as much as I have isn't magic.

It's that I started trying.

People like to say, "Admitting you have a problem is half the battle." That sounds neat, but it's generous—and it's bullshit. Admitting is only the beginning. The real work comes after.

After admitting comes the seeking; searching for ways to heal. After seeking comes the doing; the messy, exhausting, uncomfortable work of piecing yourself back together. The showing up to therapy. The journaling. The praying. The saying no to what used to numb you. The saying yes to what might save you.

Not every technique will work. But that doesn't mean you stop trying. The only thing that truly stops healing is refusing to try. I could easily blame my mom, my dad, my illness, my addiction, my ADHD, my busy schedule, or my failures. I could blame anything for not working on myself. But where would I end up then? An old woman, bitter, complaining that I never truly lived.

Fuck that.

Healing is this: showing up for yourself over and over again. Even when you're tired of it. Even when you'd rather slam the door shut and crawl under the covers. Even when you've walked into room after room, only to find more locked doors.

It can feel endless. But that's where the real work is. That's when you start to uncover your true, authentic self—the person you were before life came crashing in, before people hurt you, before shame took root in your spirit. The person you were always meant to be.

So no, my castle isn't finished. There are still rooms dark and cluttered with memories I'm not ready to touch. But there are also rooms full of laughter. Rooms bright with light and love. Rooms where joy lives. Rooms that prove I am more than the sum of my past.

Like the room where I sat on my craft table floor and cried the first time I made something beautiful.

Like the room where Bella told me I'm her emotional support mom.

Like the room where Rick held me in the ER and reminded me I'm not doing this alone.

And here's what I want you to know: the same is true for you.

Your castle doesn't have to be finished. Healing isn't about completion. It's about the courage to keep building.

I've walked you through my rooms—the dark ones, the painful ones, the ones I tried to keep locked forever. I've shown you The Room That Broke Me, The Room I Kept Dark, the Same Room with Different Addresses. I've opened the doors to rooms I never thought I'd survive, and rooms I didn't know could hold so much joy.

But here's what matters most: these are my rooms. My story. My castle. Yours will look different. Your rooms will hold different memories, different pain, different joy. The rooms you need to open might not be the ones I opened. The tools that saved me might not be the ones that save you. And that's exactly how it should be.

You get to decide which doors to open and when. You get to decide what stays and what goes. You get to decide how to furnish the rooms of your life; with forgiveness or anger, with joy or bitterness, with light or shadow.

But here's what I hope you take from my story: you can decide.

You have that power, even when it doesn't feel like it. Even when the rooms feel too dark, the doors too heavy, and the work too hard.

I'm forty-seven years old. I'm more than fifteen months sober. I'm still healing from a chronic illness. I'm still learning to be the mother my daughter deserves. I'm still figuring out how to live in my body, in my marriage, in my own skin.

I'm not done. I may never be done.

But I'm here. I'm building. And every room I open, every door I walk through, every moment I choose healing over hiding. That, in itself, is a victory.

You deserve that, too. You deserve a life that's more than survival. You deserve rooms filled with light.

So, open the doors you've been afraid to touch. Walk into the rooms that scare you. Sit with what you find there, even when it hurts. Use the tools that work for you: therapy, journaling, faith, art, community, nature, whatever gives you strength. Say yes to joy, even when grief is sitting at the table. Say no to what keeps you small, even when it's uncomfortable.

It won't be easy. Some days you'll want to burn the whole thing down and start over. Some days you'll wonder if healing is even possible. Some days you'll be so tired you can barely remember why you're trying.

But keep building, anyway.

Because you deserve a big life. A life full of light, laughter, love, and rooms that feel like home.

Your castle is waiting. And you—exactly as you are right now, broken pieces and all—are worthy of building it.

Afterword

A cknowledgments

To Rick:

You are my safe place. The room where I can finally exhale. Thank you for loving me through the messy middle, for building a life with me that I don't need to run from, and for believing I could do this even when I didn't. You've shown me what it means to be chosen every single day. I love you.

To Bella:

You are the reason I fought to break the cycles. The reason I learned to choose joy. Watching you grow into the kind, brilliant, talented person you are has been the greatest honor of my life. I hope this book shows you that it's okay to rebuild as many times as you need to. The door is always yours to open.

To my brothers:

These are my rooms, my memories, my truth. I know you carry your own. Thank you for letting me tell my story, even when our versions don't match perfectly. I love you both.

To my grandparents:

You gave me a place I could always call home. The rooms I have shared with you have mattered more than you'll ever know. Chives sends his love.

To the family I married into:

Thank you for giving me the grace to grow, to change, and to find my way. I would choose you — every time. Thank you for welcoming me as family.

To the friends who have become family:

From the theatre room to the bus station floor, to the Oldsmobile and

Mickey's Irish Pub, and all the way through to the people I spend my life with now—you taught me that family isn't just blood. You let me show up messy and loved me anyway. Thank you for the laughter, the adventures, and for always having my back. I love you all so much.

To my beta readers and advanced readers:
Your feedback made this book what it is. Thank you for seeing what these rooms could become and pushing me to make them stronger.

To Sam and Nick:
Thank you for reading my story through every stage, and helping to guide me to this final version. Your fingerprints are all over this book.

To my patients:
You trust me with your healing, and that trust has taught me more about resilience and bravery than anything else. Thank you for letting me hold your hands through the hard parts.

And to you, reading this:
Thank you for opening this door. For spending time in these rooms with me. I hope you found something here that you needed. I hope you know you're brave too.

To my mom:
I understand now.

To the readers:
If this book found you when you needed it most...

I wrote The Room to Be Brave because I needed someone to tell me it was okay to rebuild. That joy wasn't something I had to earn. That bravery doesn't mean you're not scared—it means you show up anyway.

If these rooms resonated with you, and you feel moved to share, a review on Amazon or Goodreads helps this book find the people who might need it.

And if you want to keep going—if you're building your own rooms or finding your own joy—come find me at aprildaygarcia.com. □
Sign up for my newsletter, follow along on Instagram, or just say hi. I'd love to hear your story.

— April

About the Author

April Day Garcia is a Certified Occupational Therapy Assistant, Reiki practitioner, entrepreneur, and someone who's spent a lifetime learning how to rebuild.

She is the president of The JD BUILDS Foundation, a nonprofit providing scholarships in the skilled trades to young adults, and the founder of Be Brave Travel, a business dedicated to making travel accessible for everyone. When she's not working in rehabilitation or planning her next adventure, you'll find her at her sewing machine, creating something imperfect and beautiful, or scheming up her next fundraiser.

April lives on Long Island with her husband Rick and their daughter Bella. She's been sober since 2024 and spends her days choosing joy, breaking generational cycles, and reminding anyone who'll listen that bravery isn't about not being scared—it's about showing up anyway.

The Room to Be Brave is her first book, but she's already dreaming up the next one.

For more information, visit aprildaygarcia.com or follow @aprildaygarcia on social media. April is available for speaking engagements and interviews; all inquiries can be submitted through her website.

Book Club Discussion Questions

Q uestions to Explore Together

Rooms as Metaphor

April uses "rooms" as a metaphor throughout the memoir. What rooms from your own life would you include in your story? Are there any you've closed off, redecorated, or are still building?

Feeling Unchosen

In *"The Room Behind the Velvet Rope,"* April explores being a stepchild and feeling overlooked. How do childhood experiences of being "unchosen" shape us in adulthood? Is healing from those experiences possible? What might that healing look like?

Redefining Bravery

April writes, *"Bravery isn't about feeling brave; it's about not feeling brave and showing up anyway."* When have you had to show up despite fear or uncertainty? What did that experience teach you?

Forgiveness and Healing

Throughout the book, April wrestles with whether to forgive her mother. Do you believe forgiveness is necessary for healing? Why or why not? Can healing exist without reconciliation?

Impossible Choices

In *"The Room That Broke Me,"* April reports her mother to the police at fourteen years old. Do you think she made the right choice given the circumstances? How do we evaluate "right" decisions when all options involve harm?

Recklessness and Identity

April describes her time in Iowa as *"reckless and real, and stupid and sacred, all at once."* What role does recklessness play in finding yourself? When can it be healing, and when does it become harmful?

Choosing Joy vs. Toxic Positivity

The Find Your Joy Project becomes an anchor in April's recovery. What does "choosing joy" mean to you? How is it different from ignoring pain or practicing toxic positivity?

Breaking Generational Cycles

The memoir explores breaking generational patterns. What cycles from your family have you had to consciously break? What new patterns are you trying to create?

Faith, Spirituality, and Healing

The book presents multiple versions of faith — from rigid religious rules to a deeply personal spirituality. How has your own relationship with faith or spirituality evolved over time?

Redecorating the Past

April ends the book with the idea that we all carry rooms — some beautiful, some broken. If you could go back and redecorate one room from your past, which would it be? Or would you leave it as it is?

Moments of Recognition

What did you learn about trauma, resilience, or healing from April's story? Was there a moment or chapter that shifted how you see your own journey?

One Question Left Unasked

If you could ask April one question about her story, what would it be?

www.ingramcontent.com/pod-product-compliance
Lightning Source LLC
Chambersburg PA
CBHW050446150626
46551CB00029B/1792